THE ARCHETYPAL HUMAN-ANIMAL

RUDOLF STEINER'S WATERCOLOUR PAINTING

A NEW APPROACH TO EVOLUTION

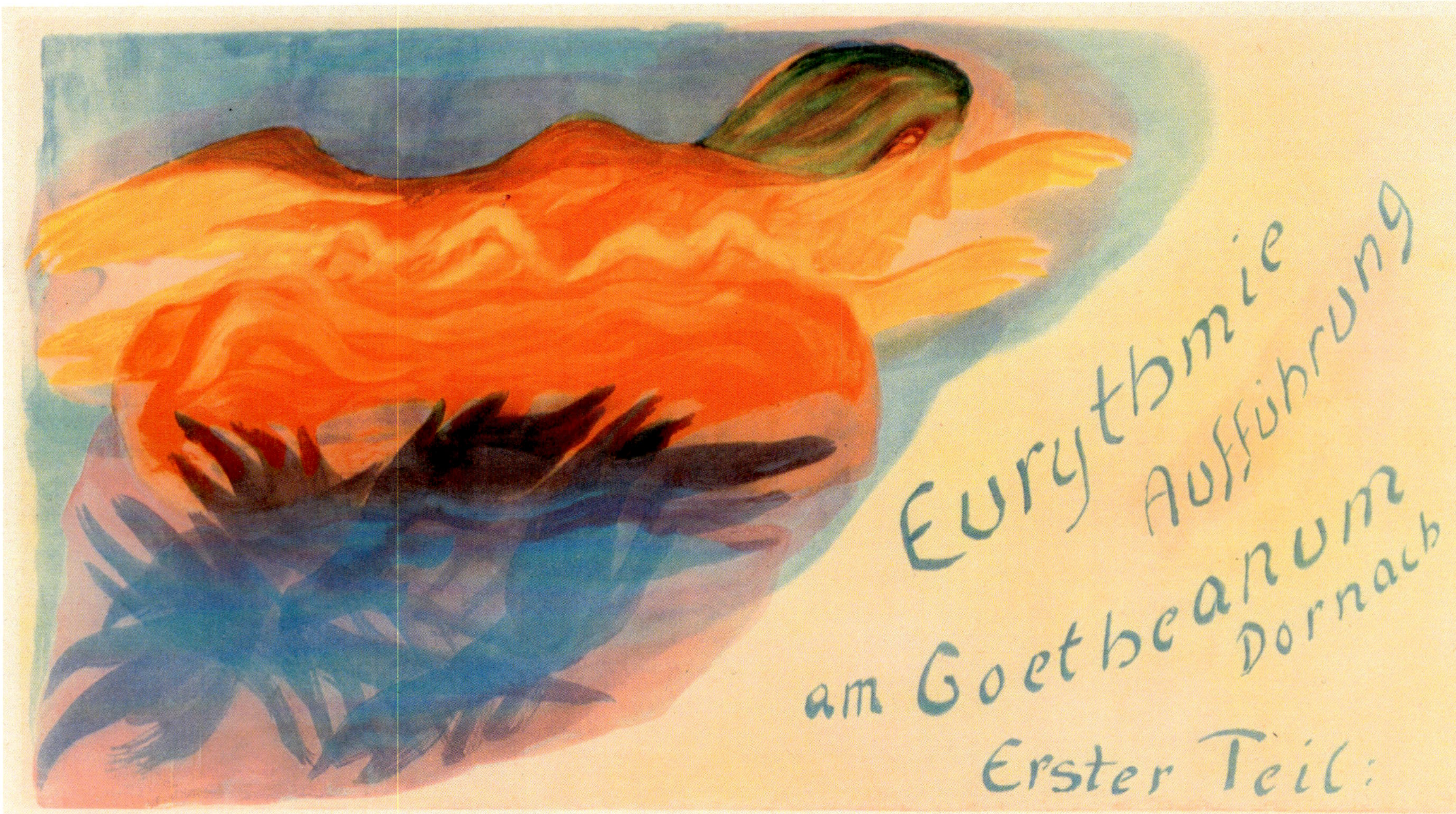

1. *'Archetypal Human-Animal' by Rudolf Steiner*

THE ARCHETYPAL HUMAN-ANIMAL

RUDOLF STEINER'S WATERCOLOUR PAINTING

A NEW APPROACH TO EVOLUTION

Angela Lord

TEMPLE LODGE

Temple Lodge Publishing Ltd.
Hillside House, The Square
Forest Row, RH18 5ES

www.templelodge.com

Published by Temple Lodge 2022

A CIP catalogue record for this book is available from the British Library

ISBN 978 1 912230 88 4

Cover by Morgan Creative
Typeset by Symbiosys Technologies, Vishakapatnam, India
Printed and bound by 4Edge Ltd., Essex

CONTENTS

PROLOGUE

'The Archetypal Human-Animal', originally titled 'Urmensch (Urtier)', was painted by Rudolf Steiner in Dornach, Switzerland, on two separate occasions, in July and August 1924. From the outset it was intended to be used as an image for a large poster advertising a eurythmy performance. In translation, the text reads: 'Eurythmy performance at the Goetheanum, Dornach, First Part'. The programme titles were cut off later when the painting was trimmed down to its present size of 132 x 77 cms.

Although the Goetheanum is named, the performance would have taken place in the neighbouring carpenter's workshop, the Schreinerei, an extensive wooden building still in existence. Here, a theatre had been created after the original wooden Goetheanum building had been destroyed by fire on New Year's Eve 1922/23.

When Rudolf Steiner was painting this image, the artist Henni Geck (1884–1951) was present, as it was painted in her studio. However, no written or verbal records exist as to how it was painted, the sequence of colours, or its actual meaning. We do know, from observation, that it was painted on a large sheet of white or off-white, relatively thin but sturdy paper, using the Windsor Newton watercolours which Henni Geck used.

Close examination of the original shows a layer of very pale crimson or carmine red painted over the whole surface of the paper as a first colour. This technique – known as a toned background – was often referred to by Rudolf Steiner as a method for painting 'out of the colour', as the colours which followed would be influenced by this colour-tone.

The image itself depicts a horizontal hovering / swimming creature with an elongated red and yellow body, a human profile and dark blue forms below. It clearly relates to indications spoken and written by Rudolf Steiner regarding early phases of human and world evolution, and the various forms which the human being embodied.

The original is stored in an archive of Rudolf Steiner's coloured paintings and pastel sketches in the Goetheanum, Dornach, Switzerland. I extend my appreciation to the curator of this collection, Dino Wendtland, for his time in allowing me to view it and for his comments.

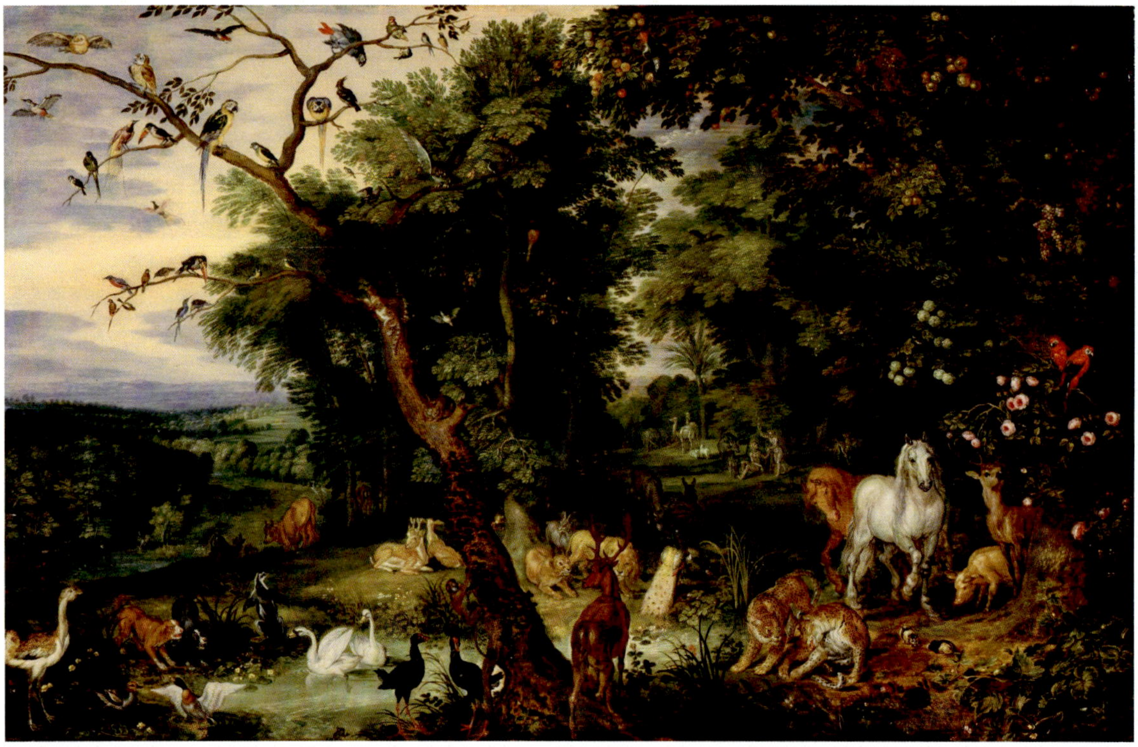

2. 'The Garden of Eden' by Jan Breugel

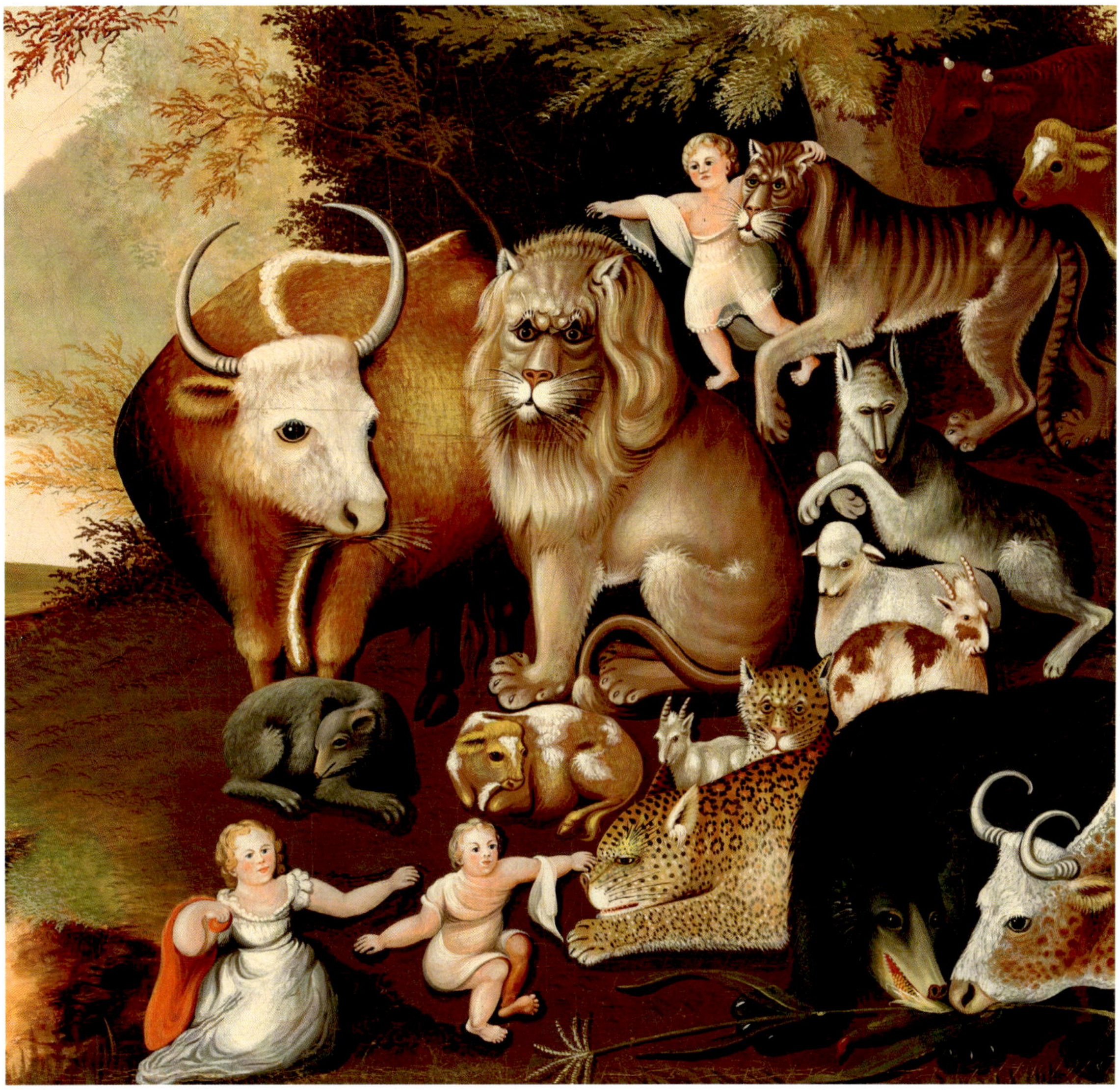

3. 'The Peaceable Kingdom' by Edward Hicks

PART ONE

Chapter One

Goethe's Archetypal Animal

'...To track down the archetypal phenomenon, to free it from other, accidental surrounding conditions, and to apprehend it in the "abstract", as we say, to me this is the accomplishment of a great and spiritual understanding of nature, and I am convinced that it represents the truly scientific aspect of knowledge in this field.'
– From a letter written by Hegel to Goethe. Feb 20, 1821

Rudolf Steiner's watercolour painting *The Archetypal Human-Animal* presents us with an enigmatic image: a strange creature appears to be swimming through water. It has a human profile, showing a clearly outlined nose and slightly-opened mouth. It has a mysterious eye, almost concealed in its greenish hair, and has appendages similar to hands and feet. Dark-blue plant-like forms float about in the water beneath the creature's bright red and yellow body.

Only the title provides us with a clue as to its meaning: it is an archetypal human-being/animal form. But even this title is enigmatic. What *is* the archetypal human-animal? What form are we looking at? What is the strange, unusual creature? We are presented with a perplexing image, and a puzzling title.

One approach to understanding this image is with reference to Goethe's* research into natural phenomena. Goethe had realised the existence of an archetypal form within the plant-world, a form which contained the essential prototype for all individual plants. He realised that all plants were the modifications of one archetypal plant (the *Urpflanze*). He also realised that it was possible for animals to have a similar unified source – that there was also an archetypal animal form, from which the different species of animals could have originated.

In his book, *Goethe's World View*, Rudolf Steiner writes that Goethe, 'wanted to discover the ground-plan by which nature forms the sequence of animals and, at the highest level of this succession, forms the human being. He wanted to find the common archetype which underlies all species of animals'. Goethe occupied himself with the writings of Aristotle on physiognomy and attempted, on the basis of his studies of organic form, to determine the difference between man and animals. 'There hovered before him the picture of a prototype which is to be found both in the animals and in the human being, which is developed in the former in such a way that the whole structure serves animal functions, whereas in the latter the structure provides the basic framework for the development of spirit.'†

---

*Johann Wolfgang Goethe (1749-1832) – poet, dramatist, natural scientist, researcher.

†See chapter: 'Goethe's View on the Nature and Development of Living Beings: Metamorphosis'.

Goethe wished to know the developmental laws of the animal forms in the same way he succeeded in knowing those of the plant. He was convinced that the unity of the animal organism also rested on one basic organ which could assume various forms in its outer structure and appearance. He discovered the developmental law of one part of this structure, namely the spinal cord and the brain, along with the bones (the skull and vertebrae respectively) which enclose these organs. He saw in the brain a higher development of the spinal cord. Every ganglion and every nerve centre represented for him a brain which had remained behind at a lower level. He interpreted or understood the skull bones which enclosed the brain, to be transformations of the vertebrae which enclose the spinal cord.

However, Goethe could not develop an archetypal image for a lawful transformation of one basic part into another for the animal form, as he had done for the plant. His essay 'Animal Form' and his 'Sketch of a Comparative Anatomy Proceeding from Osteology' written in 1795 in Jena, contain only a preliminary outline as to how animals can be compared in order to gain an overall picture of how the creative power 'produces and creates organic beings' in order to gain a norm, or a standard, by which to work out 'the descriptions', or the details. Even though he was not able to trace nature's creative force in its forming and transforming power through the different parts of the animal organism, he did succeed in finding individual laws which do adhere to the general norm or prototype, but which differ in their manifestations. In the archetypal organism all the parts are contained which can occur in any animal. In the individual animal form one part is developed whilst another part is only suggested; one part is particularly elaborated and another is perhaps imperceptible to sense observation. In the latter case, Goethe was convinced that the part of the overall archetype which is not visible in every animal is nevertheless present as an *idea*. In the archetypal animal or organism, all the parts are developed and maintain a balance with each other; the diversity of the individual organisms arise through the fact that the formative power expends itself on one feature, and therefore does not develop other fully-formed features, or perhaps only suggests them. Today, this law is known as the correlation or compensation of organs.

Goethe also sought to explain that an individual organic form gives itself a particular form related to a particular circumstance. As he tried to seek for the laws of nature and organic forms, he investigated the formative powers which the *archetypal* structure and shape were using, in order to develop a *specific* shape. For example, in order to explain a fish he examined all the different possibilities lying inherent within the archetypal – as ideas – to discover the particular forms which fish developed in order to *become* a fish. He asked the questions: 'Under what conditions does the archetypal animal become a fish?'; and 'Under which conditions a bird?'

He realised that changed living conditions stimulated the organic form to reshape itself according to inner laws. Countless forms of life are contained as idea *in* the archetypal animal – the forms which come into existence are those upon which outer influences work as stimulus. Goethe developed the concept that a species of plant or animal transformed itself into another in the course of time, and under certain conditions. It became clear to him that the shapes of living beings were not rigid and unchangeable, but are involved in continual transformation.

He wished for the working together of all the individual branches of science – natural history, physics, anatomy, chemistry, zoology and physiology – in order that a higher perception of living processes could develop. His ability to let the eyes of his spirit work together in a continuous living alliance with the eyes of the body, enabled him to see the unified sense-perceptible and the super-sensible aspects of all living beings. He could see the laws of organic development, and recognise the transformation of form. 'Seeing with eyes of the body transmits knowledge of the sense-perceptible and material; seeing with the eyes of the spirit leads to the beholding of processes in human consciousness, and to the observation of the world of thoughts, of feeling and of will. The living alliance of spiritual and bodily eye, enables one to know the organic which, as a super-sensible element, lies between the purely sense-perceptible and the purely spiritual.'*

Goethe was inspired to give expression to this living alliance of seeing both the organic physical sense-perceptible world and the realisation that a super-sensible world existed within and behind it, in his prose-poem, 'Metamorphosis of the Animals'. In this creative work he invites the reader to embark upon an imaginative journey with him as he describes his observations of the animal world. He characterises the archetypal principles which he perceives to be at work within the various animal species, shaping and forming their physical organs and giving rise to their patterns of behaviour.

* R. Steiner, *Goethe's World View,* Ibid.

Chapter Two

Goethe's Metamorphosis of Animals

'It is the story of all life that is holy and is good to tell, and of us two-leggeds sharing in it with the four-leggeds and the wings of the air and all green things; for these are children of one mother and their father is one spirit'.
– Black Elk from *Black Elk Speaks* by John-G. Neihardt

Introduction

Goethe possessed an exceptionally visual poetic gift and the power to penetrate his way right into things – into their very essence – so that everything became localised and individualised in his mind. Within him, phenomena took on dramatic, imaginative forms. His 'Metamorphosis of the Animals' provides the reader with images that are an expression of his penetrative observations of outer animal forms – how a species is influenced by different forces of nature and how it adapts to them. Logical perceptions of the animal world describe in detail the outer-forms, gestures, behavioural tendencies and responses which animals portray. Entwined with these descriptions, the glorious and mysterious being of nature, or nature herself, is revealed – her invisible presence shaped through her archetypal deeds of caring and providing.

The harmonious, trusting relationship between nature and her animal offspring is not merely instinctive, but in Goethe's mind demonstrates a finely-tuned sensitivity. Nature and the environment nurture, influence and support the multitude of forms and characteristics which animals display.

Terms with which we are all now so familiar – flexibility, adaptability, versatility – are to be found within Goethe's words, but voiced with his capacity to express them imaginatively. A gentle but profound challenge is offered to the reader – to ascend to a summit which exists both within one's own inner thought-life, and which has at the same time its expression within 'the wider field of Nature before you'. If willing to do so, the reader – as 'supreme creation of Nature' – is able to enter into the very processes and thoughts of nature herself, as they find their expression within the animal kingdom. Goethe is asking the reader to accompany him to the heights of true imaginative perception.

Goethe's 'Metamorphosis of Animals'

Now, if your mind is prepared to venture upon the final ascent
To this summit, then give me your hand, open your eyes and gaze freely
Into the wide field of Nature before you. She, the goddess has lavished
The richest gifts everywhere around her, but she is never concerned,
As are the mortal women, for the needs of their offspring
For secure nourishment. Such cares do not befit her, for she has determined
The ultimate law, in twofold wise, and has set limits to every life,

Given it measured needs, and then scattered about immeasurable gifts,
Easy to find. Calmly she encourages and favours
A variety of tasks for her children, whose needs do so vary;
Untrained, they wander on according to their pre-ordained purpose.

Every animal is complete in itself, it emerges forth, perfectly,
From nature's womb and produces perfected offspring.
All its organs and limbs are formed according to eternal laws,
And even the rarest of forms mysteriously preserves the Archetype.
So is every mouth given the dexterity to grasp its food,
Befitting each body; whether feeble and toothless,
Or powerful, with strong-toothed jaws; in every case
A suitable organ will convey nourishment to the rest of the body.
Also, every leg and foot moves, whether long or short,
Completely in harmony with the animal's intentions and needs.
Thus had the Mother ordained health, pure and whole,
For each of her children; with the limbs full of vitality,
Never contradicting each other, all working in the interests of life.
In this way does the shape of an animal determine its way of living;
And likewise, the way of living exerts an enormous influence
Back onto the shapes of the animal. Thus ordered development displays
Both constancy and a tendency to change under pressure from outer conditions.
Yet deep within the more noble creatures, one finds an inner power
Enclosed in the sacred sphere of living formative essence.
Here are the boundaries no god can alter, honoured by Nature:
For only through limitations can a form reach perfection.

However, deep within, a spirit seems to be wrestling mightily
To break through this sphere and cause the forms to be random
And the instinct divergent; yet for all he attempts, his efforts are in vain.
For indeed if he penetrates into this organ, or that one,
Making it more powerful, already in compensation other organs
Become stunted, the burden of imbalance and irregularity destroying
All the beauty of form, and all the pure litheness of movement.
So if you see any creature endowed with a particular advantage
Ask at once, what is the deficiency that afflicts it
And seek with a spirit of enquiry;
Then at once you will find the key to the world of formation.

For no animal for example, who has a complete set of teeth
In the upper jaw, has ever carried a horn on its brow;
A horned lion is therefore impossible to be composed,
For the eternal Mother however she devotes her forces

Has not sufficient material to plan complete rows of teeth
And to push forth antlers and horns as well.

May this beautiful concept of power and constraint; of caprice
And law, freedom and moderation, of movement within order,
Pre-eminence and deficiency, bring you delight and gratification;
The sacred Muse brings it harmoniously to you, gently instructive;
Moral philosophers never achieved a more sublime concept,
Nor did the man of action, the imaginative artist; Rulers,
Worthy of ruling, enjoy their crowns on this account only.
So rejoice, supreme creation of Nature, you now have the ability
To be able to rethink her exalted thoughts, the highest to which
In her creativity she has ascended. Here, stay now still and turn your gaze back,
Examine, compare and receive from the lips of the Muse
The delightful entire certainty that you do see truly and not just imagine.*

J.W. Goethe 1806

* Translated by the author with reference to Christopher Middleton's translation in Volume 1 of Goethe's Collected Works.

PART TWO

Chapter One

An Evolutionary Background

'Yet druids hint of long Atlantean years where cloud and vapour gloomed, and day was night. So seldom did a sun-gleam cross a life, whole ages deemed the sun no more than a dream, a legend, or a sheen of a passing god.'

– 'Within Her City of the Golden Gates' by W.P. Ryan

The earth has developed, together with humanity, through various states of evolutionary progression, and in earlier phases of earth's evolution it appeared in a very different form than it does today. We as human beings have also developed. In our distant past we had a very different appearance. This has been revealed through Rudolf Steiner's clairvoyant spiritual-scientific research and detailed descriptions can be found in many of his writings and lectures. Through orthodox research methods we can learn only a limited amount about our early, pre-historical existence, as archaeological evidence, palaeontology and geology provide limited information, and historical texts, inscriptions and records shed light only on a few millennia. Even with hard 'physical' evidence, theories regarding our early evolutionary phases remain flexible. With each new discovery established, ideas are challenged when new evidence reveals hitherto unknown pieces of a vast evolutionary jigsaw puzzle.

Through his thorough spiritual-scientific clairvoyant investigations, Rudolf Steiner was able to penetrate the Akasha Chronicle which contains, in its spiritual substance, the living script – or living pictures – of all past world events. He was thus able to 'see' and to 'read' the images which contained the records of earth's primordial beginnings and its early evolutionary phases.

His book entitled *Cosmic Memory, Atlantis and Lemuria*, written in 1904, contains the outcome of this research and provides remarkable details of his spiritual investigations. He describes clearly and vividly the appearance of the earliest stages of human evolution at a time when we, humanity, were not yet physically embodied, but existed as ensouled astral substance. Rudolf Steiner wrote that, during an early stage of earth's development, there was no material separation between the sun, the earth and the moon – they were joined as one mass of delicate substance.* Firstly, the sun withdrew its substance from the common heavenly body, and received its task as light-giver. In the human being, the sense of seeing developed, but not as we know it today.

---

* See the Appendix.

Light and darkness acted upon the human being as vague sensations. For instance, under certain conditions we experienced light to be pleasant, and strove towards it. At the same time, our soul life continued in dreamlike pictures; coloured images, which had no immediate relation to external objects, arose and vanished. The human being connected these coloured images to spiritual influences. Light images appeared when we were affected by pleasant soul influences; dark images when we were touched by unpleasant soul influences. Gradually, as the new instruments, or organs, of sight developed, the light impressions from the outside were more intimately connected with our own inner soul life. The outside world became mirrored, or reflected, within the soul as image. The human 'body' condensed into an incredibly delicate 'wateriness', with the heat-ether coursing through it. This 'wateriness' gave the body a substantiality which could be called gas-like or mist-like, similar to a fine (but still invisible) astral cloud floating in the air. It could move to all sides by means of limb-like organs and is referred to, in mystery science, as the stage of fire-mist. This human being could still impregnate itself and reproduce beings without external influence – in other words, there was no separation of the sexes.

Humanity existed in the condition we could refer to as 'pre-Paradise', in an undivided unity, but in a condition so rarefied that we would not be able to see it with our present sight. After many aeons, the earth and moon separated, allowing a further evolutionary phase of development to unfold.

This stage of world evolution which Rudolf Steiner refers to as 'Earth evolution', involved stages of development which were recapitulations, i.e. on a new level of previous stages of development. I quote:

> The astral ancestors of humanity were brought to the etheric earth. They absorbed refined etheric substance into themselves, thus developing etheric bodies. These had an elongated elliptical form, in which the limbs and other organs, which were to be formed later, were already indicated by delicate shadings of the substance... All processes were regulated by the soul... They shared in the life of everything pertaining to the soul in their environment... The actions of stones, plants and animals, which then existed only as astral [soul-like] forms, were felt as inner soul experiences.*

This phase of development was given the name of Polarean – or, in theosophical terms, the first root race of our earth. In a later stage of development, known as the Hyperborean phase, human forms appear in soft malleable shapes, carrying the nature of man and woman within themselves. Every human being could produce another human being out of itself. The consciousness was dreamlike, and the most developed organs at that time were the organs of motion. The whole 'body' was composed of a rarefied substance, not even as dense as our present air; but it could hear, having a delicate perception of cosmic sound, and it could sense changes in the outer temperature of the surrounding ether world. Nature and the

---

* *Cosmic Memory*, Chapter Eight: 'The Hyperborean and the Polarean Epoch'.

developing human being were still intimately connected – whatever was taking place in the surrounding outer world was influenced to a large extent by the forces of this early human-animal being.

Sounds were also experienced at an early stage of these creature's lives, as emanating from the spiritual beings who surrounded them in the spiritual worlds. Towards the end of their existence, they could no longer hear them outwardly, but they became inner memories through which they felt united with the Angels. Towards the end of their lives, they could imitate them. This sounding or singing, in imitation of the spiritual beings which they had heard, created a great activity in the watery element of the earth, forming mighty waves and surges of water within the earth and over its surface. They could perceive other living beings around them through the warmth, light and sound effects that they produced. Our being contained within itself both the human and animal natures – there was no separation at this time of the later physical, soul and spiritual differentiation into the human and animal kingdoms.

But not all the human-animal beings were alike. Some developed distinctive head forms (which we see in Rudolf Steiner's painting) whilst others developed appendages to assist their movements through the air-water substances. There were, in fact, three distinct types of human-animal at this time. The image in the watercolour painting seems to depict all three types combined into one. Some evolved the beginning of what afterwards became the form of the head; these were, the most harmonious in their inner life, having a strong inner connection to the Spirits of Form (the Exusiai). The second type developed more prominent appendages and became more deeply involved in the 'earth' world, being more dependent on external conditions. They were aware of belonging to the spiritual worlds through the light-effects of the Spirits of Fire (Archangels). The third type of human-animals were full of eager impulses for action, for activities which were possible in the conditions prevailing at that time, especially for movement. They had a stronger relationship with the Angels and developed a more prominent 'bodily' nature, with more distinct organs and rudimentary 'limbs', or hand and foot-like appendages.

The consciousness of the human-animal, as stated before, was one which existed in a dreamlike condition, but in a deeply harmonious connection to the spiritual hierarchies, whose presence protected and guided their development. Even the activity of their breathing was directed by higher spiritual beings (who dwelt within the sun); they guided the streams of air which permeated the 'physical' body, and breathed life into it.

We may wonder, at what stage of evolution did our archetypal human-animal begin to become differentiated into the two separate kingdoms – the human and the animal? The gradual separation of the human being from the animal nature took place as a result of various processes.

We will consider these processes and remarkable events in diverse ways and from different aspects to provide insights to the early and extraordinary phases of our evolution.

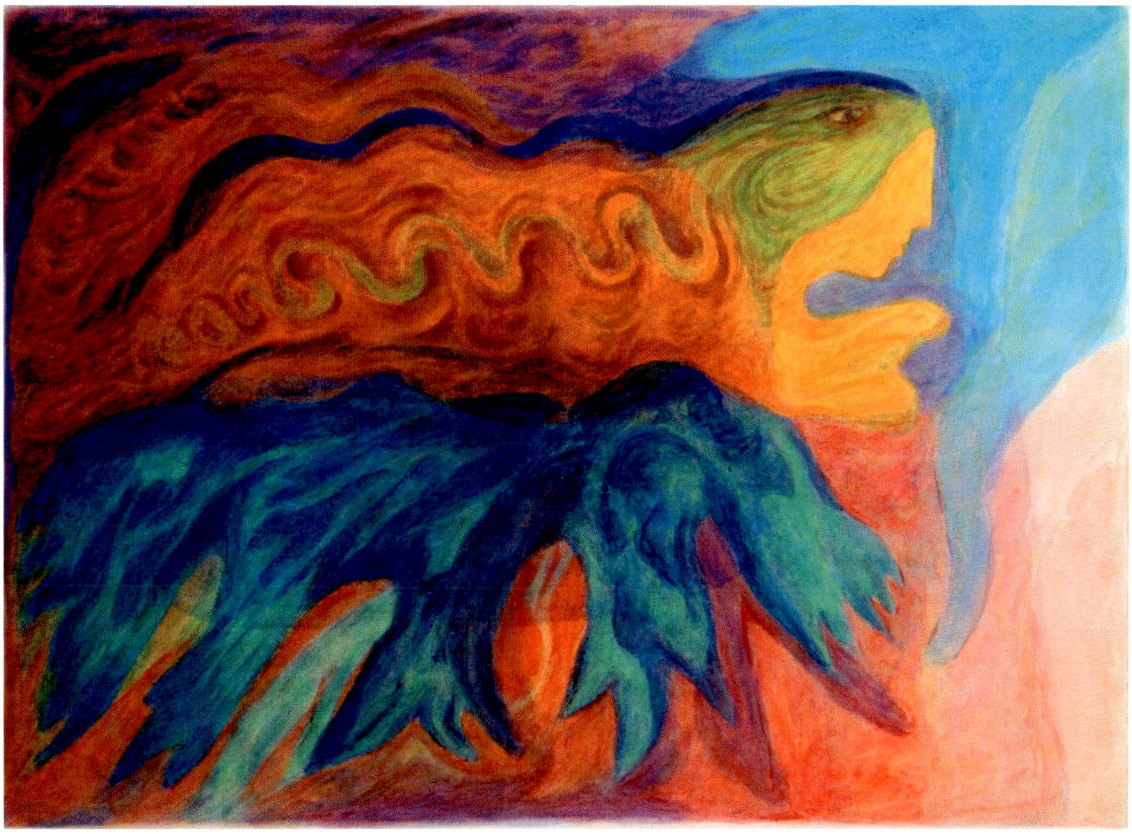

4. 'Large Archetypal Animal' by Gerard Wagner

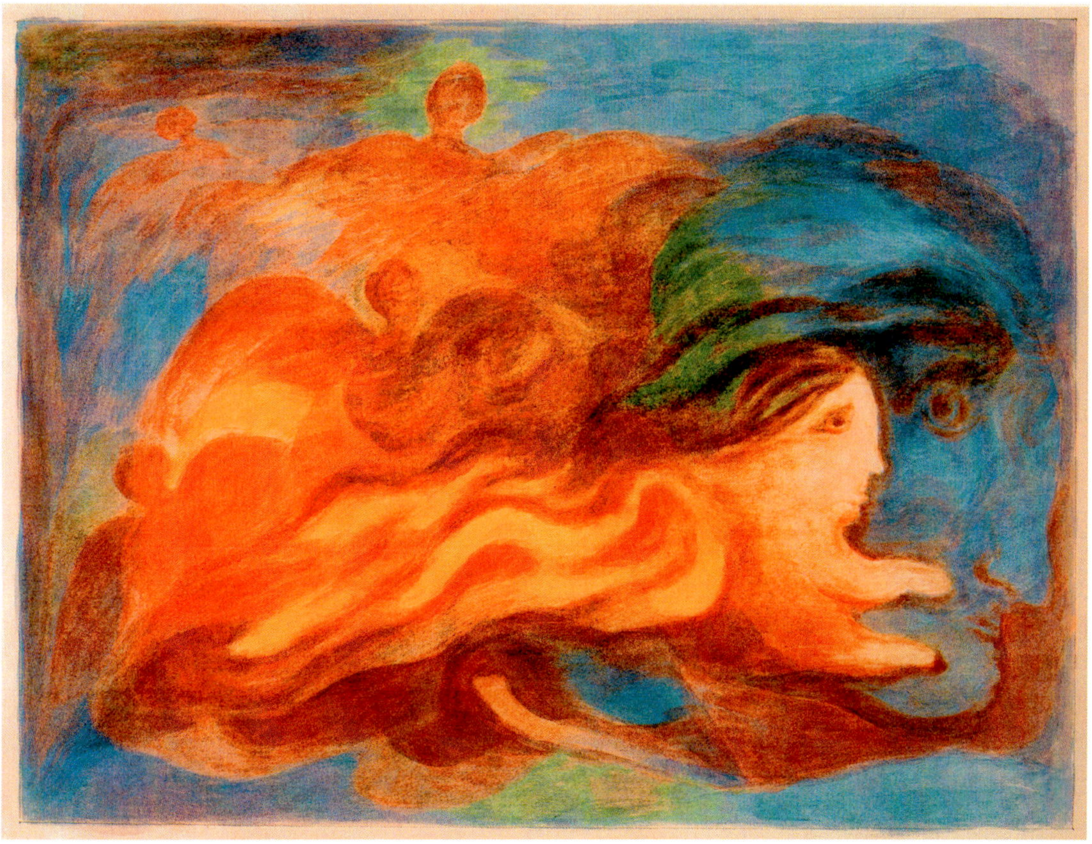

5. 'Archetypal Animal' by Gerard Wagner

Chapter Two

The Human Being on Ancient Moon: the primal beginnings of Archetypal Human-Animal

'Earthly dwelling place and cosmic home are the two poles between which all evolution progressively evolves.'
– Herman Popplebaum

The ground mass of ancient moon, the moon phase of our evolution, was formed of a semi-live substance, which was sometimes sluggish, sometimes quick and lively. This was a kind of plant-mineral kingdom. It was penetrated by a second kingdom consisting of a kind of plant-animal, which was softer and more mobile than the ground. The human being could be described as animal-human. They had in their nature the constituents of the other two kingdoms, seen from a 'physical', clairvoyant point-of-view. But the human being was permeated by a life body (an etheric body) and an astral body, upon which the forces of the hierarchies on the sun were working to gradually ennoble. The Spirits of Form bestowed a form adapted to the moon life; the Sun Spirits elevated the human being to a higher level.

A twofold nature began to develop. That which was influenced by the moon beings was more independent and our ancestors felt themselves to be an 'image of the universe'. Influences from the sun made them feel themselves as 'images of the sun' only. Alternating states of consciousness came about, according to the strength of these two influences.

There was great variety at this time, with the mineral-plants differing from one another, group by group; as did the plant-animals and the human-animal.

As time went on a whole number of heavenly bodies detached themselves from the moon 'body', so that a whole system of heavenly bodies existed, with the sun being the most advanced.

Our Astral Body : Food, Pleasure and Pain

Advancing in their own spiritual development, Spirits of Personality (the Archai) could work upon the human astral body, and Fire Spirits (the Archangels) upon the etheric. Our ancestral 'bodies' could now experience pleasure and pain, and gained the character of 'personality' through relating these sensations to themselves through their astral body.

The surrounding gaseous substances were gradually being condensed to watery substances and a kind of nutrition took place: what was received from without was inwardly transmuted and assimilated. If we imagine something intermediate between the nutrition and breathing of today, then we have an idea of this process. The human being derived 'food-stuffs' from the animal-plants, which floated or hovered in the surroundings, or were sometimes loosely rooted in the ground. A kind of pleasure was experienced when helpful substances were absorbed; discomfort was felt when harmful substances flowed in.

As well as this process of nutrition, there was also a breathing process, an in-drawing and out-pouring of warmth. Organs could open and close, allowing a warmth-giving stream to pour in and out of them, so that air and water substances were conveyed inward and outward. Both breathing and nutrition were accompanied by inner feelings.

Our Consciousness : Dreaming and Shaping

We lived within a vapour-like environment, with manifold processes taking place within it: substances were combining, separating, condensing and thinning out. We could sense all of this, and it created pictures – or dreaming-images – in our consciousness, which were not arbitrary but related to what was happening. These images were able to arouse our whole inner life to movement and action – they were formative forces in reality: we *became* in response to their forming us. We became, in a way, an image of our own processes in consciousness. Within these images we sensed the world around us, as well as the spiritual beings creating it: the Spirits (the Archai) the creatures of the animal-like kingdom; the Fire Spirits (the Archangels) behind and within the mineral-plant beings; the Sons of Life (the Angels) as ethereal soul forces.

The power proceeding from the picture-consciousness grew gradually less and less able to extend over and through our whole bodily nature, and we divided into two co-joined parts, into two different natures.

The Duality of Body and Head

After an interval of rest, human beings were divided into two forms. One withdrew from the working of the picture-consciousness, taking on a more definite shape and coming increasingly under influences streaming in from the sun beings. The other rose out of this one, like a kind of head. It was mobile and pliable, shaping itself to express and sustain the dreamlike consciousness in which they were living, but the two portions were intimately connected, sending each other their respective fluids. A rhythm of cosmic influences came about; sometimes the moon forces were stronger, sometimes the sun. The senses did not yet transmit impressions of external objects, but at this stage they reflected the beings of the Sons of Life, the Angels. A whole group of human beings felt themselves to belong to one Angel, who had its existence within the airy-watery-cloudy surroundings.

Cosmic Music

When the influence of the sun was stronger, our astral bodies experienced cosmic harmonies, and became as though a delicate and wonderful musical instrument upon which the chords of cosmic mysteries resounded.

Certain parts of the astral body were shaped and formed in accordance with the harmonies of the universe – the tones of spiritual, cosmic sound. All this was taking place in the middle phase of the moon evolution.*

* See further in Rudolf Steiner, *Universe, Earth and Man*, Lectures 5 & 6.

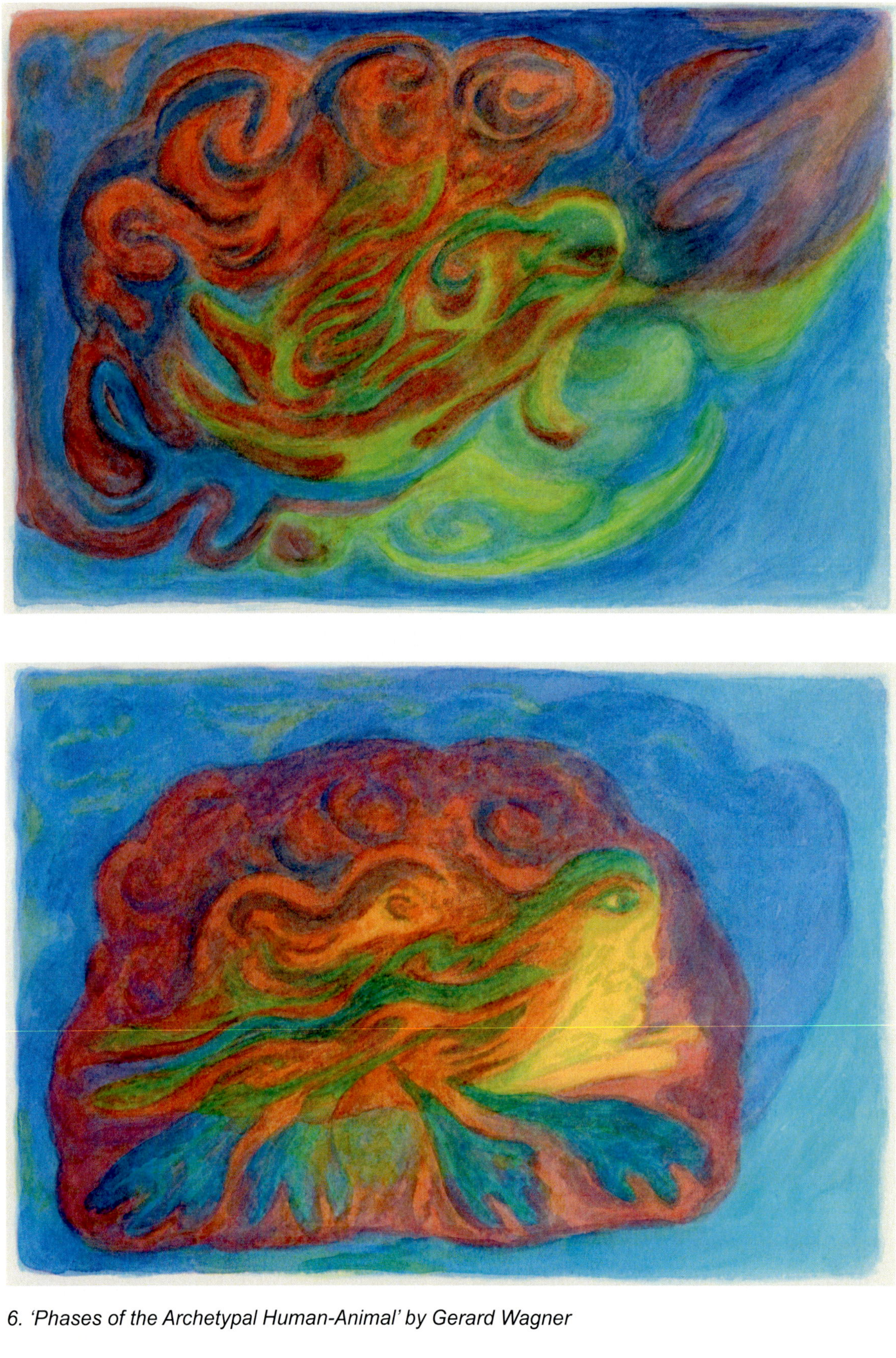

6. 'Phases of the Archetypal Human-Animal' by Gerard Wagner

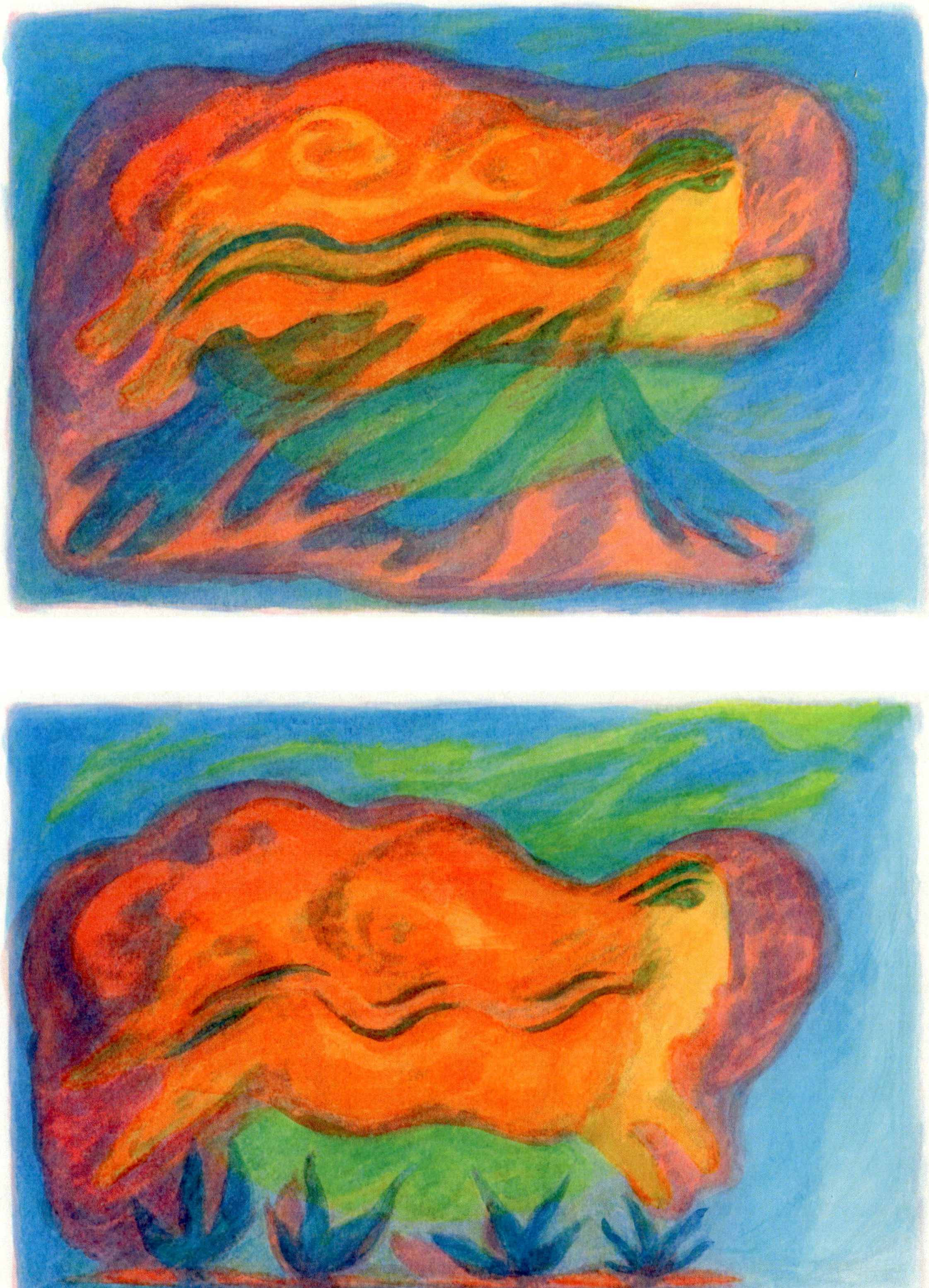

7. *'Phases of the Archetypal Human-Animal' by Gerard Wagner*

PART THREE

Chapter One

The Human Being: Handiwork of the Gods

'What a piece of work is a man! How noble in reason! How infinite in faculty! in form and moving, how express and admirable! in action how like an angel! in apprehension, how like a god!

– from *Hamlet* by Shakespeare

The human being is complicated. We consist of our physical body, etheric body, astral body and ego. These four principles play into one another in a very complicated manner.

If any being in our physical world had only a physical body, it would be a stone, a mineral. A being possessing a physical body and an etheric body has a plant-nature; our whole plant realm consists of these beings. Animals are beings which have physical, etheric and astral bodies; and a being which, in addition to these, also possesses an ego, is at the stage of *human* existence on earth.

Which of these four principles is the oldest? It is the physical body which initially was formed as a body consisting only of warmth during the ancient Saturn phase of evolution. When we consider our present constitution, we observe our solid skeleton; fluid constituents of many kinds; the air which permeates us, and our inner warmth.

If we think away everything solid, liquid and airy and imagine warmth only, we have what was present on ancient Saturn, which consisted of forms of warmth. These were the original foundations of the human 'body'.

After a period of rest (a pralaya), Saturn changed into the sun formation, which consisted of warmth and air. The human being now had a 'physical' body of warmth and an etheric body of airy substance, but different from our present air, being much finer.

In this sun phase of evolution we glittered and shone with varied colours, sparkling in the most wonderful way. The entire, vast sun-globe consisted of shining warmth-air bodies. It was the human being who, as part of the sun, radiated the illuminating power of light into space. Our physical body of warmth taking into itself the etheric body of air, became luminous.

After a further period of rest, the sun gradually passed over into the moon phase of evolution. The airy formation gradually condensed into a vaporous watery one. The ancient moon was actually a delicate fluid body. Here we can find physical human bodies consisting of fine flowing fluids in which currents of air coursed, just as breath and warmth intermingle in our bodies today.

At this stage we assimilated an astral body, consisting of a physical warmth body, an airy etheric body and an imperceptibly fine delicate 'fluid' body – an astral body.

It was during the moon phase of evolution that the sun (far greater in its existence and size as the sun we know of today) departed from the combined earth-moon, together with the most advanced spiritual hierarchies.

Humans now dwelling within the earth-moon stood midway – in consciousness – between the present human being and the present animal. They were guided and directed by exalted sun-powers.

In the middle of the moon phase we do not find our present clearly defined kingdoms of nature, but intermediate combinations: we have a human-animal kingdom, an animal-vegetable kingdom and a vegetable-mineral kingdom.

On our present earth we walk upon solid ground; the beings of the ancient moon moved upon what was the lowest kingdom of the moon – the vegetable-mineral – which was half alive. We can think of a mossy, spongy bog or boiled spinach – a kind of mush, but living and bubbling. There were no rocks, but something like dense woody vegetable clumps which later condensed and hardened to become our present rocks.

From out of this vegetable-mineral substance grew the animal-plants, which had a certain degree of sensation when touched. Animal-human, however, consisted of the finest substances, and hovered above the spongy earth. The physical body had a very strange appearance: it was still soft and fluid, with an animal-like head formation from out of which the etheric and astral bodies projected and extended. All these animal-human beings had various forms which recall our present animals, but they only remind us of these. For when viewed with the astral vision of a clairvoyant person, the higher nature of this animal-human could be seen as having an inner pictorial consciousness, similar to our present dream-consciousness. These inner pictures, or images, were meaningful. For example, a certain image would indicate that something harmful was approaching, whilst another would indicate that a friendly or compatible being was near.*

Following a pralaya, or rest, after the moon phase of evolution we reach the earth phase where, initially, the earth and moon were united as one large intensively active mass. Following on from the Polarean and Hyperborean stages, from the Lemurian epoch to the middle of the Atlantean epoch, the human form was gradually constructed. When the Lemurian evolution was in its prime, neither such a breathing system nor a system of digestion existed such as we have now. Substances were quite different; respiration and nutrition were in a certain sense connected – they performed one common function which was only divided later.

Our very ancestors absorbed a kind of watery milky substance which supplied them with substances for both respiration and nutrition at the same time. Human beings still moved within the fluidic element, and could differentiate between warmer places and colder areas. This was made possible through an organ which has since become atrophied, namely the pineal gland. At one time it was an active organ, opening outwardly from the head and sending forth rays. Human beings moved about in the watery element with a kind of lantern which developed a certain light, and which enabled cold and warmth to be distinguished. It was the first universal sense organ. It was also, in these

---

* See R. Steiner's *Universe, Earth and Man*.

ancient times – before the division of the sexes – an organ of fertilisation. When the earth and moon were still united and the sun stood in a certain position, the atmosphere of the earth provided a substance which caused this organ to shine. Human beings could absorb substances from the environment which made them capable of bringing forth new 'bodies', re-creations of their own.

Sense perception, fertilisation, nutrition and breathing were all intimately connected in this primeval phase.

The pituitary gland also regulated the functions of nutrition and respiration under influences from the moon, both before and after it withdrew from the earth. The pituitary gland enabled the activity of shape-shifting, when human beings could inflate themselves and change shape. This activity was voluntary. Less voluntary alterations depended on the pineal gland. Influences, and a wisdom-filled instinctive consciousness similar to that of our present-day animal kingdom – a kind of dreaming-thinking – flowed into humans at that time from the hierarchies in the spiritual worlds who were guiding their development.*

Rudolf Steiner's clairvoyant research throws further light onto the mystery of the human being. He wrote that at this stage of the human form, in the early Lemurian time: 'It converted one half of itself with two out of its four organs of locomotion into the lower half of the body, whose chief function thereby became the nutritive and reproductive activities. The other half was directed upwards and the two remaining organs of locomotion were stretched out as fin-like hands. And those organs which had previously aided nutrition and reproduction, began changing into organs of speech and thought.'†

---

* See R. Steiner's *Occult Science*.

† From the journal *Lucifer Gnosis*, 1905. No. 19-33.

Chapter Two
From Fire-Air to Air

'Where the flame cannot live, no animal that draws breath can live.'
– *The Four Elements*, Leonardo da Vinci

At the moon stage of evolution the gaseous air-substances of the sun phase had densified so far as to produce a pulpy, thick-ish fluid flowing mass of which all the beings, including animal-humans, actually consisted. We can imagine this as the white of a hen's egg – somewhat thickened – and into this substance of the human being, the nervous system was incorporated.

This phase of the moon (in which the earth was included in its mass) was surrounded by a warm atmosphere permeated by watery substances, known as fire-air or fire-mist. This was breathed by the beings of the moon, who had no lungs. Even the highest beings, the animal-humans, breathed through something similar to gills, as present-day fishes do. We could say that our distant forefathers on the moon breathed 'fire-mist'. This was known by the alchemists of our Middle Ages, who could bring elemental beings into their service by creating similar misty, fire-air substances.

The smoky, steamy warm atmosphere was at times interpenetrated by currents which hung down from the air like soft cords, permeating the human 'bodies'. These could be likened to cosmic navel-cords through which the human 'I', which was in the peripheral surroundings, conveyed substances in and out. Angels, or Folk-Soul spirits, assisted the flowing substances, the precursor to our present blood, to flow through the 'I' and into the soft body structures.*

This created groups of souls who were connected, as different Angels passed on their influences into their own groups. This created the very beginnings of what much later would become the various broad groupings of humanity.

The moon human-animals hovered and circled above and around the soft moon surface, moving in a similar way as our present water creatures move in water. At certain times, when the moon was in a particular position to the sun, the human-animals could sound out their germinating power into the cosmos. A cosmic event was finding its expression. This was the first sounding of inner tones as expressions of the soul. Relics of this are preserved in the calls of certain animals, wolves or stags for instance, when they howl or bellow in mating seasons, or when dogs, wolves or coyotes howl during a full moon-phase.

After a time, when all the beings of the moon existence had passed through their evolution and could ascend to higher stages, the sun and moon reunited and entered into a resting phase, a pralaya.

Then a new existence shone out, the earliest phase of earth, beginning with a short recapitulation of ancient Saturn, sun and moon. During this time ego-consciousness

* See R. Steiner's *Cosmic Memory*.

was incorporated into the astral, etheric and soft 'physical' bodies, but this took place through a somewhat complicated process. Firstly, in the Saturn recapitulation, the earlier forms of sense-organs were worked upon by the higher beings related to light, to sound and to smell, so that these could receive the ego. Then, during the sun recapitulation, the tree-like forms and currents which formed the solar plexus organ, the glandular organs of growth, reproduction and nutrition, were further worked upon so that they could receive the ego. Thirdly, the moon recapitulation developed a further growth of the nervous system so that the ego could be received.*

With the departure of the moon out of the earth, significant changes were taking place: the spinal nerve-cord became vertical in contrast to the completely horizontal position which it had during the moon period. Soft spinal marrow came up into the brain. During the moon and moon-recapitulation phases, man needed a kind of swimming 'bladder', similar to our present fishes. This was part of the human constitution, allowing and supporting the floating swimming motions. As the surrounding air changed, the swimming bladder gradually transformed into lungs. From a gill-breather, man became a lung-breather.

This metamorphosis is expressed in the Bible as: 'And God breathed into his nostrils the breath of life and man became a living soul.' Here is expressed what had taken place in the human being over millions of years.†

* See R. Steiner's *Theosophy*, Chapter 'Evolution of Mankind on the Earth'.

† Ibid. Refer also to the time-charts in Appendix 2.

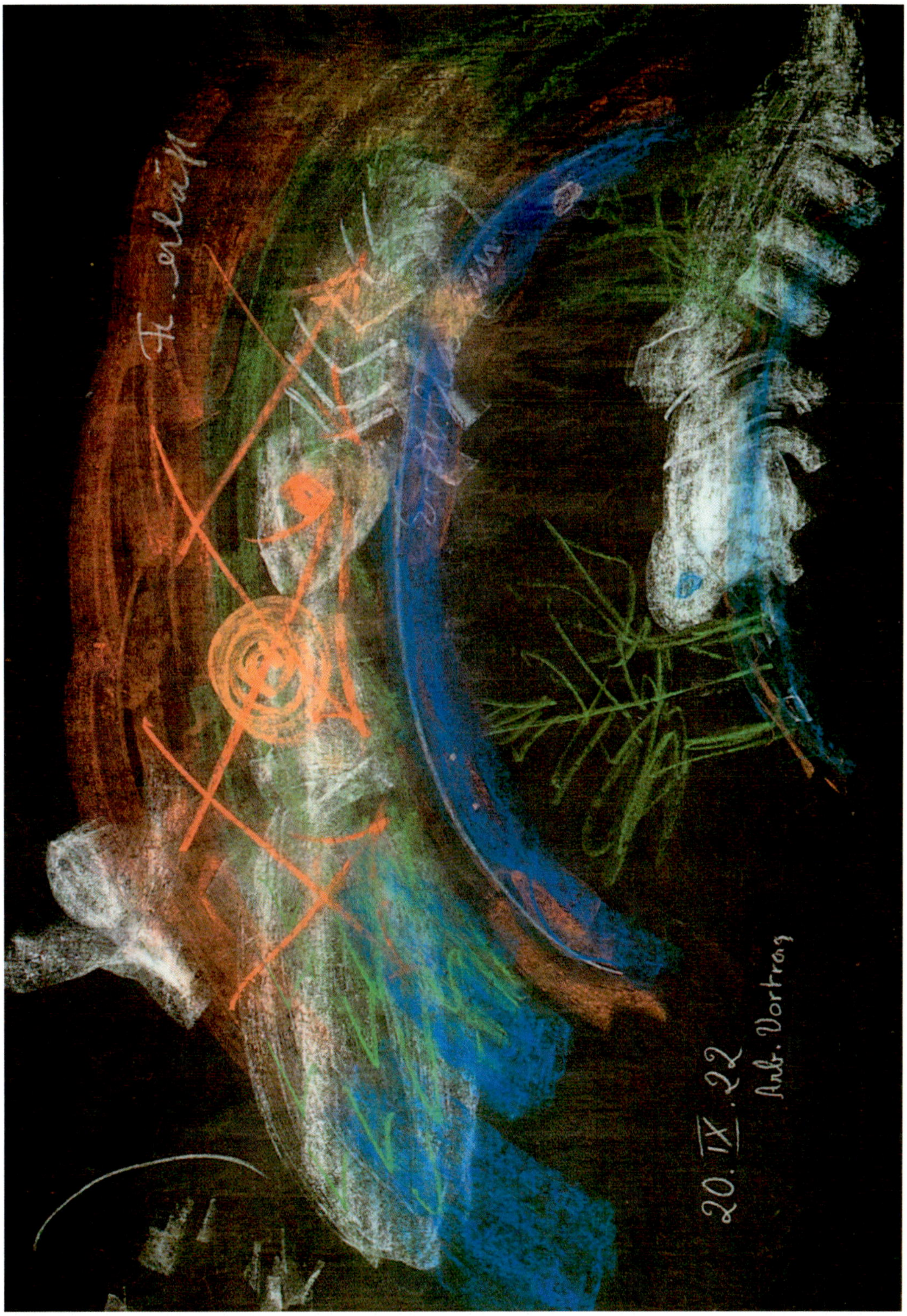

10. 'Lemuria' by Rudolf Steiner

PART FOUR

Chapter One

The Animals: From the Cosmos Down to Earth

'If you wish to say that the shells are produced in nature in these mountains by means of the stars, in what way will you show that this influence produces in the same place shells of various sizes, and varying age and of different kinds?'
– Leonardo da Vinci

When we look at the wonderful variety of animal life around us, we begin to question how this diversification came about. When we consider the earliest forms of animals, it is clear that differentiation began relatively early, already in Palaeozoic times, when fishes, amphibians and reptiles were distinguishable. But long before this, when the earth was still soft, certain animal prototypes existed.

Rudolf Steiner once said that, during the Hyperborean period, the earth was so vast that it extended as far out into space as the sun is today. However, the earth then was neither solid nor fluid, but was of a warmth-light consistency, and the processes taking place occurred in quite different ways. This youthful condition of the earth was vigorous, turbulent and revolutionary, involving organic structures of such plasticity that they suddenly appeared and just as suddenly vanished again.

Steiner then described the Lemurian age as a stage of development during which the earth was like a thick broth:

> The mountains we know today were still dissolved in it. The earth was a lump of fairly thick sauce in space. In it floated giant oysters… These oyster-like creatures consisted mainly of a gelatinous substance but wore a hard armour as do our present day turtles. We could say they were the precursors of the forming of the earth's crust. To us it all appears to have been gigantic because we ourselves have shrunk so much. The earth today is old, small, hard and disintegrating. However, it was not always so; it was once filled with life and activity such as we can hardly imagine.*

During this early malleable life-filled phase of earth's development, the animals were being formed. How did the different species come about? When we gaze upwards into the starry night sky, we recognise the zodiac – Greek for 'circle of animals'.† It is here that we find the animal archetypes manifested visibly in the star-clusters, once seen as

* Quoted from Karl König, *The Animals and Their Destiny*, Chapter II.

† In the German language, *Tierkreis* = animal circle.

living spiritual entities by ancient clairvoyant humanity, who perceived the archetypal forms and gave them their names.

Each star sign has spiritual divinities dwelling within its realm. Rudolf Steiner explains that: 'If we direct our gaze to a certain direction in space, occult vision perceives something quite different in one direction from what it sees in another. Space is no means homogeneous, for diverse forces work from the various directions of space. The whole of cosmic space is filled with spiritual beings of the hierarchies working in different ways from different directions onto the earth.'*

Certain folk in the past, who had a far deeper sensitivity for these things than we do at present, were aware that definite and precise forces streamed down from certain places from cosmic space which are of particular significance to the earth. They were aware, for example, that when a specific planet moved through the different signs of the zodiac, this brought about a streaming down of formative creative forces which influenced the forming of a particular animal-type. When a planet stood before, say Aries, Taurus, Capricorn or Cancer, the creative forces were such that a particular animal-form could be moulded or shaped accordingly.†

We mustn't forget, however, that all earthly substances were volatile, softer and more pliable than is the case now. We might consider, for example, that if Mars stood before Leo, then certain forces could work down upon the archetypes of the lion forms on earth. Or, if a planet moved across Taurus, then the cattle, the ruminants, were given their archetypes. A planet moving across Capricorn sent down forces to influence what would become the extended goat family; a planet crossing Pisces created the primitive precursors of the fishes, and so on.

It also mattered where each planet stood in relation to the sun, so that the formative influences were manifold and varied.

The mighty spiritual beings of the Spirits of Motion, the Dynamis, created the group-souls of the animals.

> We can, in a certain sense, describe the animal group-egos as offspring of the second Hierarchy... For that which we call the I, the ego, can only be found within the animal kingdom on the astral plane in the supersensible world; there, only it has the centre of its activity. Occult science cannot ascribe an ego (an individuality) to the animal in the physical world... The animals do have their soul-forces, their extraordinary intelligence, their wisdom and quite wonderful comprehension on the physical plane, so that on earth their behaviour can be likened to that of humans... but in the animal only three principles are active on the physical plane, the physical, etheric and astral bodies, while the wisdom-filled group-ego is on the astral plane.‡

---

* From *The Spiritual Beings in the Heavenly Bodies and in the Kingdoms of Nature*, Lecture IX.

† Ibid.

‡ Ibid, Lecture IX.

A gradual separation took place, with humanity becoming slowly more bound to the earth – the animals also finding their homes upon the earth but their group-soul, their true ego-being, remaining in the cosmos, while the human ego was gradually descending:

> In the animals dwell spiritual forces belonging to beings not to be sought upon the earth itself, but outside the earth in cosmic space, and indeed primarily in the planetary world. The Regents, as it were, of the principal group-forms of the animals, live on our planets; they had to withdraw into these planets in order to work down with their forces at the right distance from the earth and from the right direction. For only from these directions in space can come that which builds up the principal animals in the right way.*

We can ask, then, how it is possible that so many diverse animal forms have developed? Rudolf Steiner states that initially, in far distant times, there were only seven principal forms, which were so soft and malleable that they were easily transformed. This took place gradually over aeons of time through the cosmic processes of the relationships existing between these planetary Regents and the spiritual beings of the zodiac.

In conclusion, we can ask whether the marvellous animals depicted in cave paintings are memories of these archetypal forms? Painted as if hovering in a magical realm, weightless and superimposed one upon another, they seem to float in a space other than the earthly. The natural clairvoyance of early humanity, combined with their remarkable artistic skills, have left an earthly record for us to behold and to wonder at, thousands of years later. Do they depict shamanistic rituals, or hunting magic? Or, do they represent supra-earthly archetypes embodied in earthly animal forms, an acknowledgement of a cosmic origin?

---

* Ibid.

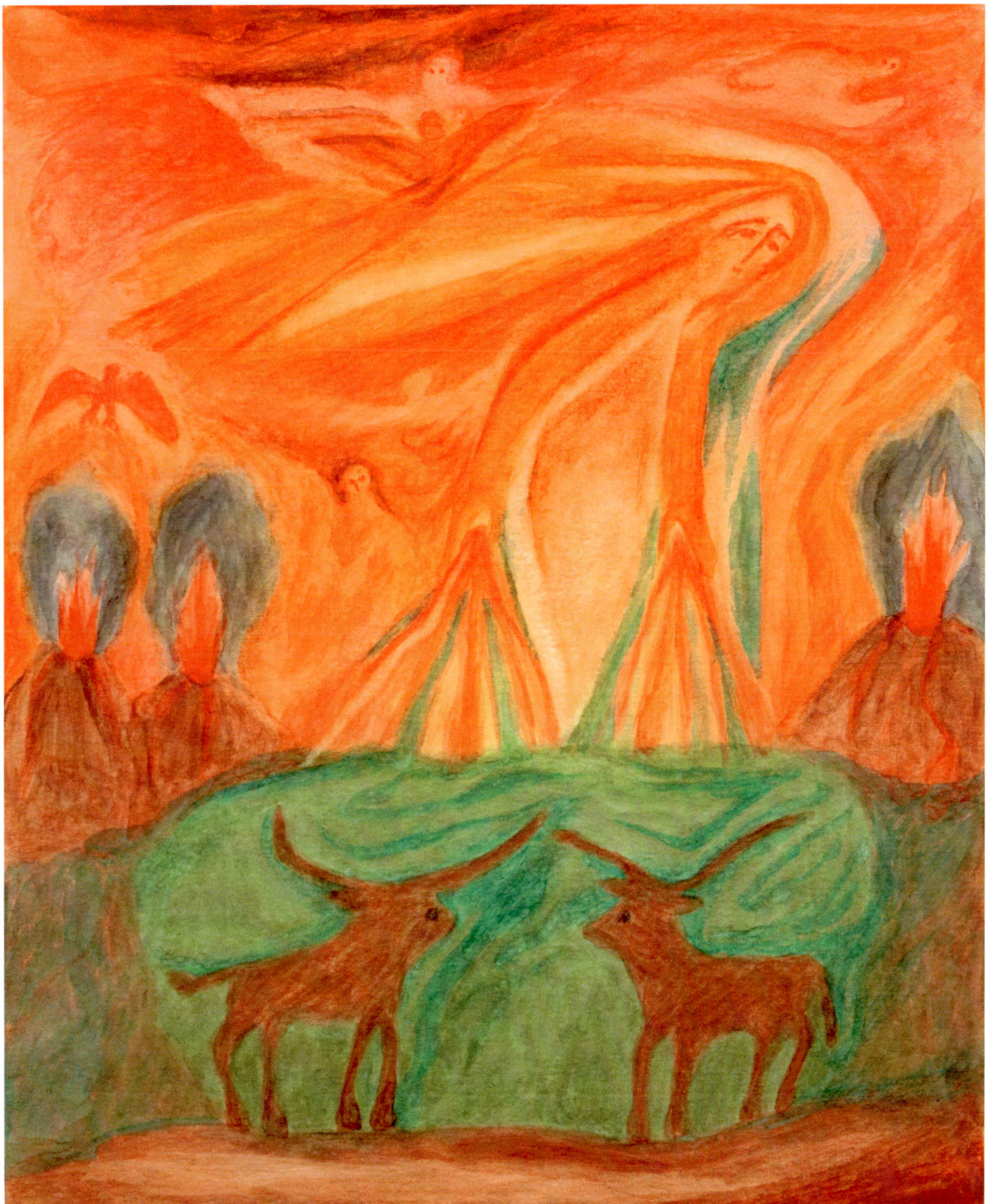

11. *'The Bovine Archetype' by the author*

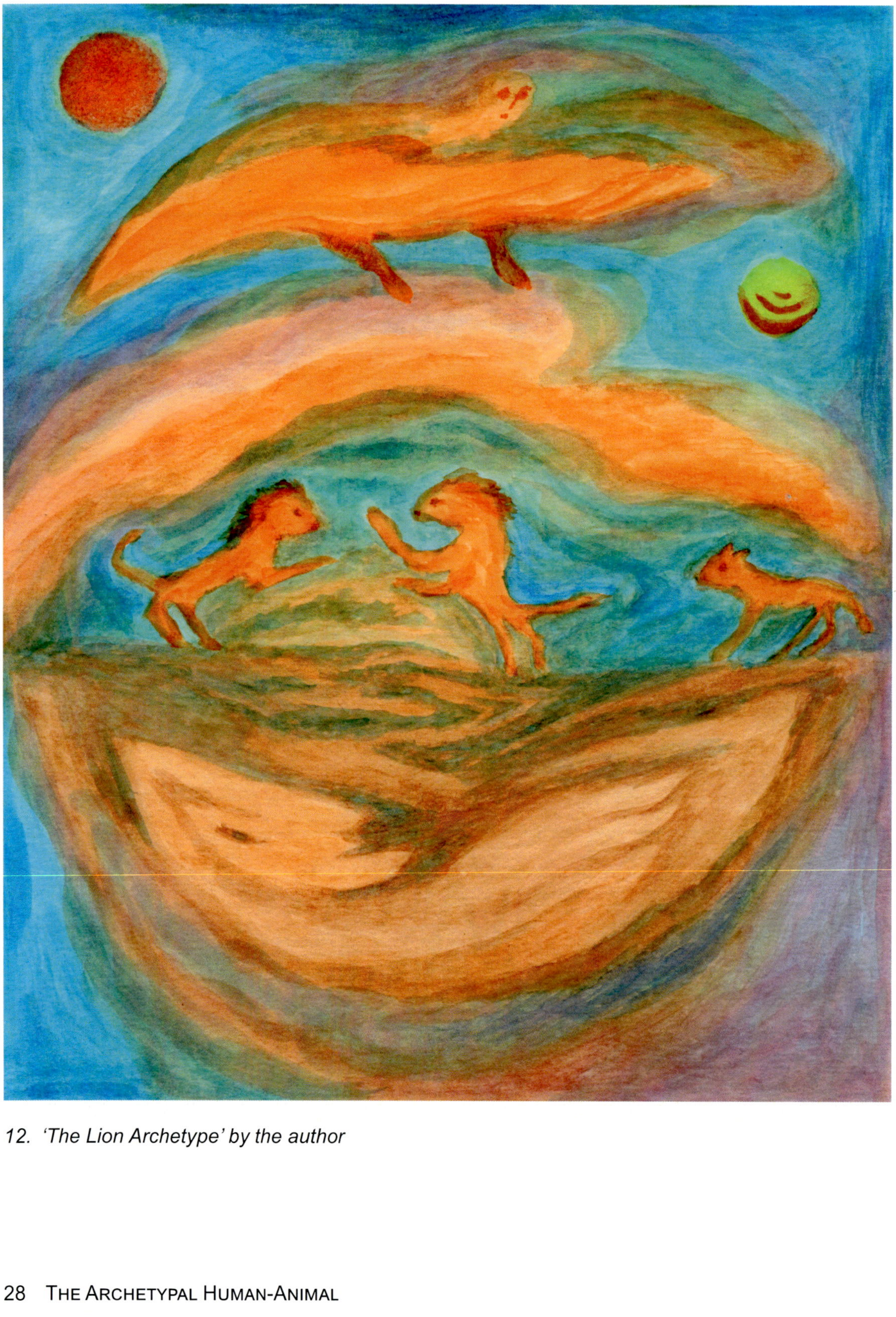

12. *'The Lion Archetype' by the author*

Chapter Two
The Origin of the Animals

Little Lamb who made Thee?
Dost Thou know who made Thee?
Gave Thee life and bid Thee feed
By the stream and o'er the mead;
Gave Thee clothing of delight
Softest clothing woolly bright;
Gave Thee such a tender voice
Making all the vales rejoice:
Little Lamb who made Thee?
Dost Thou know who made Thee?
– From *Songs of Innocence and of Experience* by William Blake

During the later stages of the Lemurian epoch, the earth was beginning to harden. This affected the soul of the human-animal too strongly, resulting in the number of human forms on earth steadily decreasing. Forms began to appear in which human souls were not incarnated – forms which were able to receive only astral bodies.

While the earth was becoming emptier and lacking in human inhabitants, these astral beings were now establishing themselves on earth. A similar occurrence had happened earlier; during the time when the sun, moon and earth were all still united as one vast mass of spiritual substance, there were also souls of forms which had to be deserted by human beings. These were the forefathers of the animal kingdom, and in the course of time they evolved organs of movement, which in the human being only existed as appendages. This is how the animals originated. They had souls which lived in many forms together, what we could call a 'group' soul – one soul existing in many outer manifestations.*

During the time in which the moon separated from the earth, when the earth had been hardening too rapidly, the volatile and inhospitable conditions on earth were such that only a small number of human souls were able to survive. They incarnated into bodies composed of pure, flexible, soft substances, which they could shape according to their wishes.†

However, other souls were uniting too strongly with physical substances that were less pliable. They were craving to return to the earth from the cosmos, where the majority of souls were dwelling. These souls, led by their longing and their impatience, made earthly bodies prematurely. The earthly bodies were bound into definite and defined forms too hastily, before they were able to be permeated by the etheric – or life – forces.‡

* See Rudolf Steiner's *Occult Science*, Chapter Four, 'Man and the Evolution of the World'.
† Rudolf Steiner, *The Gospel of St John and its Relation to the Other Gospels*, Lecture 5.
‡ Ibid.

Lacking the flexibility of the etheric forces, in the course of time these bodies could not be reshaped into new forms suited to ongoing human development. They lagged behind, remaining in a variety of stagnant forms, which gradually condensed and hardened into animal forms. This occurred through the late Lemurian period, corresponding to the Mesozoic era.*

Atlantis

In the early Atlantean epoch we also find our ancestors in a very different condition than our present one. They consisted of a soft substance, having no trace of our present hard bones – nothing even as solid as cartilage. They swam in the watery air, which was still permeated by fluid; they were a kind of 'water being', hardly distinguishable from the surrounding water. The etheric body projected on all sides beyond the physical body, especially around the head.

The physical body was soft and pliable, and could be changed at will. Throughout the early and middle Atlantean epochs, human beings had great power over their physical bodies. If they wished that a part of their body – which later might become a hand, for example – should be lengthened, then this was possible. They had the capacity to move their limbs, to lengthen them and to inflate themselves, increasing in size.

During this stage, certain beings freed themselves too early, and did not allow the divine spiritual activity to further their characteristics. These beings then became fixed in certain forms which later hardened and condensed into the whole range of the present animal kingdom. If we ask whether human beings originated from such animal forms, the answer is, no. Human beings remained above the surface of the earth, in the purer elements, and only solidified when the time was ripe to do so. This point of time, when our ancestors descended to earth, is beautifully portrayed in the Biblical legend of Adam and Eve in Paradise. However, Paradise was never upon the earth but above it, as human beings only descended from Paradise – from the spiritual worlds – to earth after they had received their definite form – although very different still from the traditional artistic depictions of this profound event.

In evolution, nothing is repeated, every stage having its particular mission in the great household of cosmic existence. When observed clairvoyantly, the earth can be seen as a place or dwelling full of beauty and wisdom, inhabited by humanity in order to fulfil its development. The most spiritual aspect of human nature, the true ego or individuality, was bestowed towards the middle of the Atlantean epoch, when the true human form was gradually appearing.

The warmth of the blood was necessary for the development of the ego. Individual life could not begin until this stage was reached. With every physical breath, not only air was breathed in but also the surrounding spirit, which had descended upon humanity. The higher spirit, which dwells within the warmth of the blood, had also descended. The ego, the 'I', was bestowed, and this was followed by the capacity to give it a voice. Thus, speech developed, and towards the end of Atlantis the human being could say, 'I'.

---

* See Appendix, Table of Geological Time.

The animals would never be able to do this. Their sounds, each so distinctive according to their species, give the wonderful variety and richness to our surrounding natural world, whilst providing them with their own unique ways of expression and means of communication. These are sounds which echo their ensouled nature – as enchanting as bird-song, as mighty as a lion's roar, as mysterious and mystical as whales' singing below the waves. These are the soundings, the many voices, of the animal kingdom.

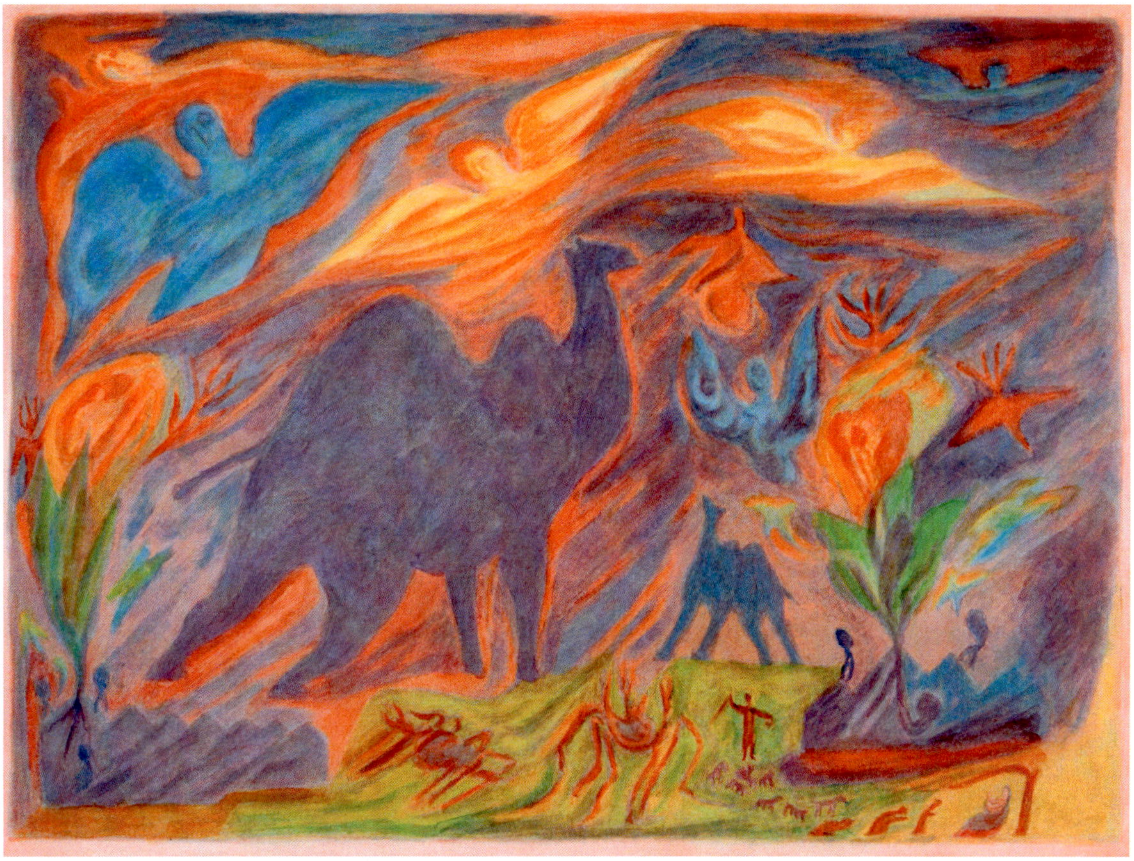

13. 'Lemuria' by Gerard Wagner

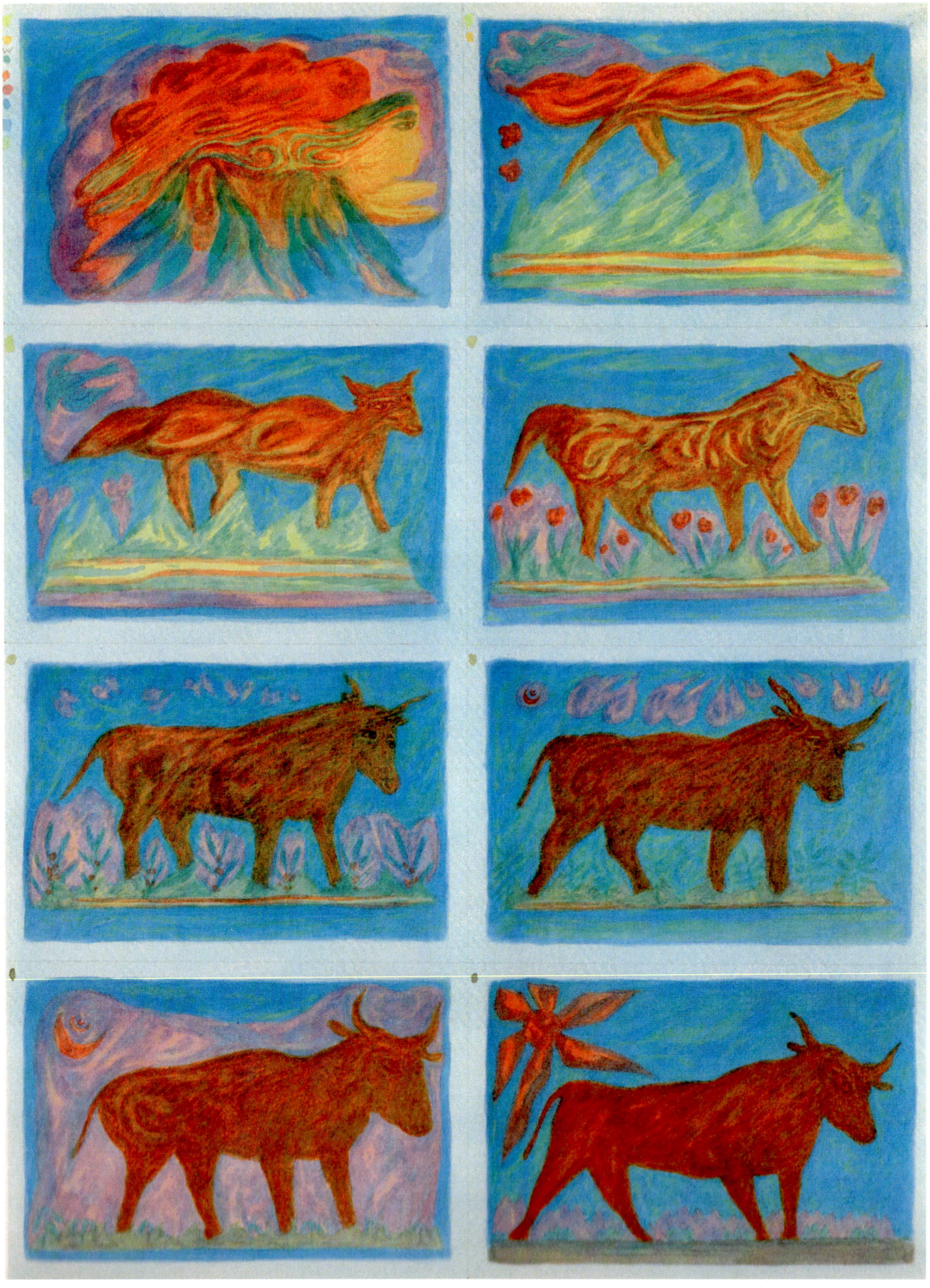

14. 'Archetypal Animal Metamorphosis II' by Gerard Wagner

Chapter Three

The Human-Animal Plant Becomes Human

'The significance of a person is not what they attain but what they long to attain.'
– Kahil Gibran

A final aspect to consider is the inclusion of plants within the development of human beings. Rudolf Steiner's painting depicts not only the animal and human gestures, but also the plant kingdom. When we look at the painting, we see that on the lower left-hand side there are dark-blue forms. These represent plant structures, and are similar in form to algae or seaweed (kelp). We then see a pictorial imagination of a threefold combination of human, animal and plant, united together in Steiner's painted image.

This chapter looks at some of the evolutionary phases of the plant kingdom in its relationship to human evolution, and the necessity of our having to cast it out, as we also needed to do with the animal kingdom.

In the earliest Lemurian phase there appeared gigantic floating plant formations similar to our algae, which floated in fluid albumen, taking their nourishment from it. The plants could shine, cast light and vanish; appear again, shine and vanish. They were capable of changing to such an extent that this arising and disappearing was possible. The plants seemed to appear out of the cosmos like airy clouds, condense and then dissolve, which is indeed how the plant kingdom came from the cosmos down to earth. When the plants were visible and shining, the albumen was green, as our present earth is green during spring and summer.

Cosmic forces also worked upon the aluminous substance in such a way that certain portions of it coagulated. These were forms of living creatures – animals which consisted of coagulated albumen which solidified to a gelatinous state, similar to gristle. They had giant, soft forms similar to our present (although much reduced in size) reptiles and lizards.

Silica and later calcium substances were also coming into the earth, which eventually hardened into crystal structures and into limestone respectively. The chalky calcium substances were attracted to the gelatinous gristly albumen and it filled them, actually impregnating them and eventually creating the animals with calcareous bones, which gradually came into being during the later Lemurian epoch.*

Other processes were also taking place. The sulphurous atmosphere was gradually being permeated by oxygen, giving strength to the soft, aluminous forms of the human beings. This gave humanity the forces to cast out both the plant and animal forms. Why was this necessary? Human beings were not only instruments of the gods, but slowly developing a more independent will, which could come about through the process of casting out the vegetable-animal substances. By casting them off, humanity rid itself of this superfluous matter, allowing the will to become a quality of the soul.

* See R. Steiner, *Mystery Knowledge and Mystery Centres*, Lecture 4: 'The Relation of Human Beings to the Earth'.

If all these products had remained within, they would have taken over the will forces, which would have become a physical manifestation only. Now, gradually, humanity could develop a freer, independent expression of will as an aspect of the soul.*

A second human faculty was developed later – the capacity for a more independent feeling in the soul, which would prepare humanity for earthly existence. How did this come about? The human being needed to discard its connection with the gigantic creatures that then existed. Some creatures were half swimming, half floating in the thick atmosphere, and had a large eye-like organ – a kind of lantern-like formation on their heads, surrounded by an aura radiating light and warmth, with an adjoining snout protruding forwards. Their bodies were lizard-like with powerful wing-like fins. Other creatures had heavier limbs – more reminiscent of today's mammals – that moved about as swamp-creatures in the soft marshy pleasant-smelling earth.† Humanity also needed to cast-off these huge animal creatures so that a freer feeling-life in the soul could grow. This took place in the period connecting the Lemurian with the Atlantean age.

A third discarding process also needed to take place in order that humanity could develop an independent thought life. How did this take place? Towards a later phase of Atlantis, the substances of carbon, oxygen and all the various metals gradually developed, which in turn gave rise to a further development of plant and animal life. These plants and animals were similar to those of our present time – but humanity in Atlantis was more intimately connected to them. As this environment was coming into existence, the human race was being prepared to live on earth as thinking beings. Between one earthly life and another, we experienced a spiritual existence in the spiritual worlds. It was in this realm, in the planetary spheres, that human beings could free themselves from their connections with the plant and animal kingdoms during the later Atlantean epoch.‡

It is through these three 'casting out' phases that we evolved into what we are today; thinking, feeling and willing beings who depend on our physical constitution on earth, and who have, in the course of time, gradually separated from the plant and animal kingdoms which surround us externally.

Through this process of separation we have furthered our own evolution, and the plant and animal kingdoms have metamorphosed into their present forms. We do however remain in an evolutionary condition of being completely dependent upon our natural environment: trees provide the all-important oxygen (and other trace substances) which we need to breathe; plants give us our food and nourishment and flowers give colour, beauty, perfumes; and animals have provided transport, clothing and food whilst assisting us in farming and agriculture, and even accompanying us into war! They also give us comfort and company in our domestic lives.

All that we have cast away in the distant past continues to provide us with life and sustenance. The casting-off process which allowed the archetypal human-animal to become human need not necessarily be a process of rejection, of exploiting and of

* Ibid., Lecture 5: 'The Mineral, Vegetable and Animal Creations'.

† Ibid., Lecture 4 & 5.

‡ Ibid.

harming as it is at present, but one of respect, care and co-existence. In the past, nature worship was celebrated through sacred and reverential rituals in cultic practices that stemmed from a profound awareness of nature's divine origins and interconnectedness. It was a knowledge of human beings existing as microcosms in relation to world existence as a macrocosm. Divine spiritual beings, gods and goddesses, directed and spiritually accompanied the initiated leaders, priests and priestesses in sacred ceremonial practices that acknowledged, in a deeply profound understanding, the symbiotic and co-dependent relationships existing within the spiritual and the physical.

The path of human freedom is ancient and on-going. Love, gratitude and humility are not mere sentiments within our human soul in our relationship to the whole of natures' realm, but the very core of our future existence.

> We are created from the spirit;
> tree, flower, corn
> insect, fish, animal –
> all are born
> in order to sustain
> growth and life.
> To destroy for gain
> to wreak havoc and strife
> has been the price
> of our freedom.

However, a new freedom can be gained:

> The light of the sun is flooding
> The realms of space,
> The song of the birds resounds
> Through realms of air,
> The blessing of plants spring forth
> From the being of the earth
> And human souls rise up
> With grateful hearts
> To all the spirits of the world.*

This lovely verse embodies an attitude of soul for a healthy contemporary relationship to nature. It can be enhanced through the knowledge of our divine past working into the present, and through acknowledging the world's archetypes, as voiced in the following two verses:

> There has arisen from its narrow limits
> My self and finds itself

---

* From the Prologue of Rudolf Steiner's first Mystery Drama, *The Portal of Initiation*.

As revelation of all worlds
Within the sway of time and space;
The world, as archetype divine.
Displays to me at every turn
The truth of my own likeness.*

In secretly to feel
How all that I've preserved of old
Is quickened by a new-risen sense of self:
This shall, awakening, pour fourth cosmic forces
Into the outer actions of my life
And, in becoming, form me into true existence.†

* R. Steiner's *Calendar of the Soul*, Verse 6 (12–18 May).

† Ibid., Verse 38 (24 –30 November).

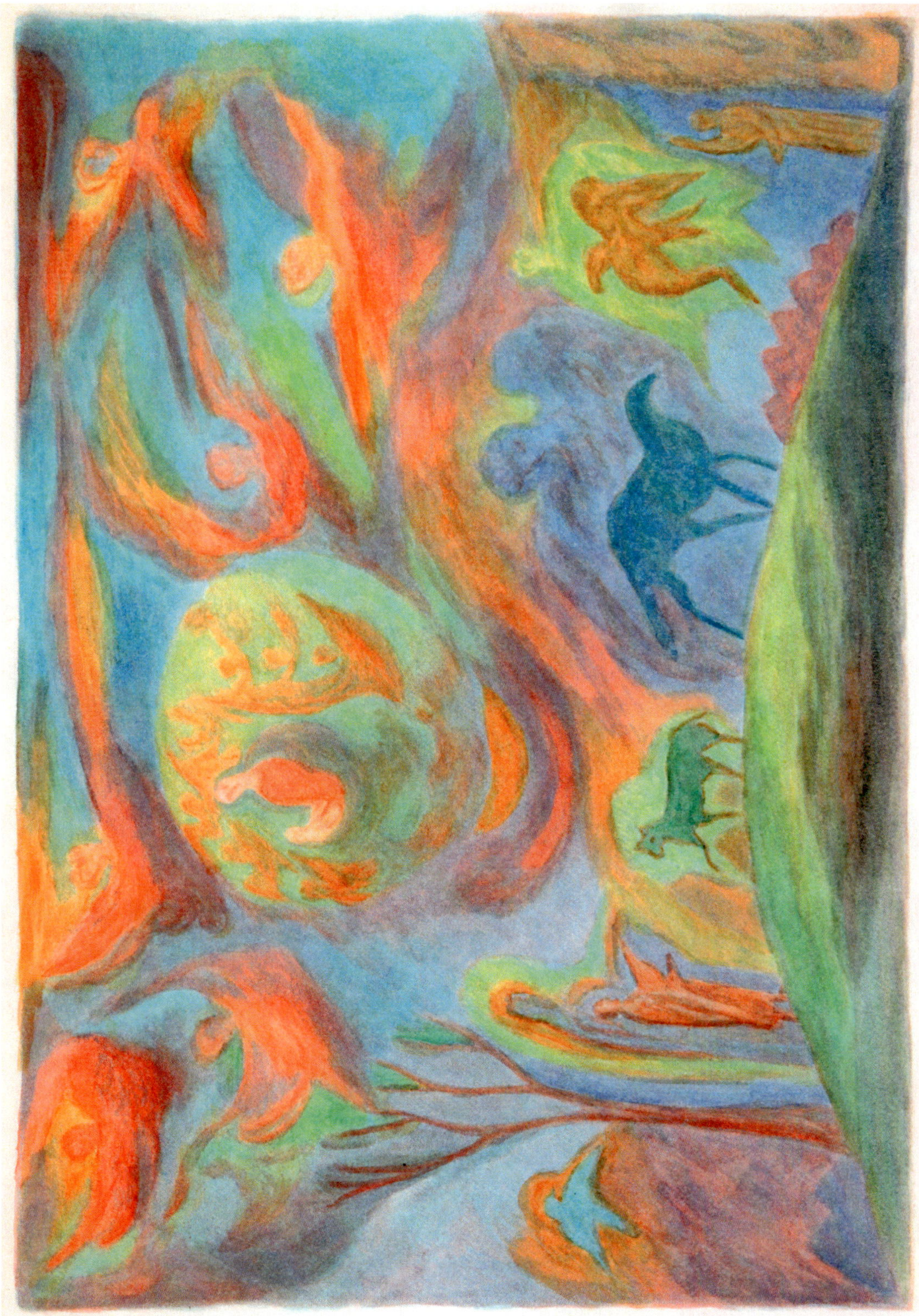

15. *'In the Animal Realm II' by Gerard Wagner*

PART FIVE

Chapter One

Myths and Legends: Monsters and Mermaids

'Many an evening the sea-maid sisters rose up together over the water. They had splendid voices, more charming than any mortal could have… When a storm was approaching… they swam on before the ships and sang lovely songs, which told the sailors how beautiful it was at the bottom of the sea…'

– 'The Little Sea Maid' by Hans Christian Andersen

Many different cultures – from a wide range of times and from a far-flung variety of places – all share common mythological themes. One such theme concerns legends about beings and creatures associated with water – from great supernatural gods and goddesses to monsters of the deep. Many include stories of mermaids (and, less commonly, mermen) – the alluring half-human being, whose lower body is that of a fish and upper half that of a human.

In order to form a fuller picture of the 'Archetypal Human-Animal' theme, we can look at some of the many legends which contain fascinating descriptions of water beings, and the different ways in which they have formed relationships with humans – from the terrifying to the romantic; from the benevolent all-protecting, to the vengeful and destructive. Bearing in mind that the primordial human being was naturally clairvoyant, and had at one time remarkable faculties of memory which extended back through a direct ancestral lineage, we should acknowledge that folklore has its origins in perceptions which were far-reaching rather than far-fetched… Each legend contains elements of truth; relevant and meaningful within the context of its original source. Veiled, embellished references to some of the descriptions, which were later verified by Rudolf Steiner and other clairvoyants,* fill the myths with a rich sense of ancient substance, providing us with sometimes delightful, sometimes bewildering images of humanity's past.

The marriage of mythology and spiritual-scientific research is a union which can clarify the otherwise obscure and opaque content and imagery of the mythological world. The perplexingly complex layers of events and the extraordinary range of creatures and characters – both natural and supernatural – which create, occupy and play their roles within mythology, can be elucidated and understood a little more readily if we are prepared to extend our consciousness just a little bit further.

* Edgar Cayce, for example.

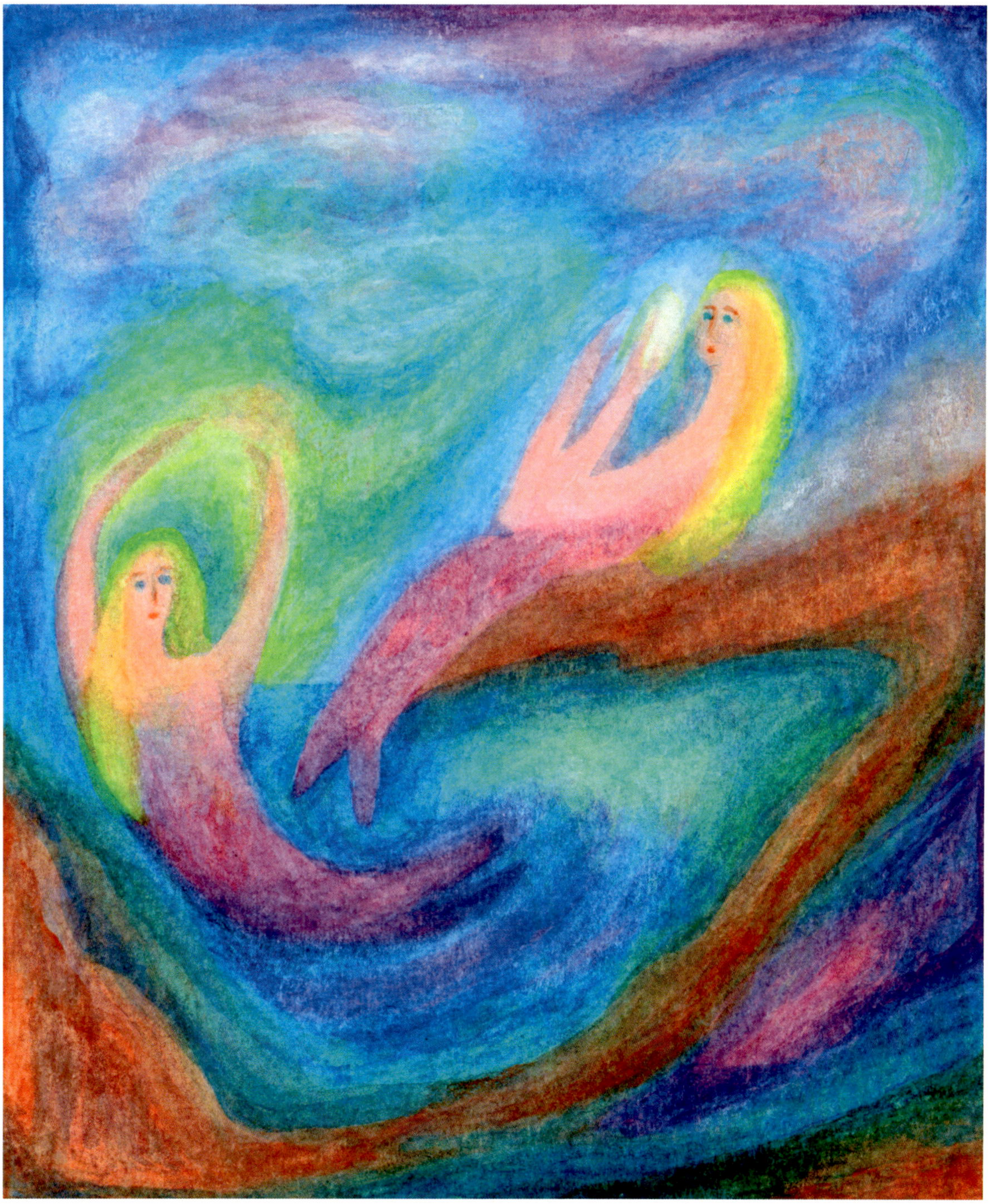

16. 'Mermaids 1' by the author

The psychological aspects of mythology have been extensively explored and charted within the context of psychology, analysis and therapy. The symbolic, representational aspects have also long been established and accepted. But what if, concealed behind the surface of these legends, there are memories of real events, real beings, and real relationships? What if they are not symbols, but actualities? If we are able to remove some of our modern cynicism, our contemporary intellectualism, and to work at a process that requires a synthesis of research, belief and keen observation (both in a visual and imaginative sense), we can begin to form the capacity to enter into these wonderful myths and legends in a deeper way. They comprise the dim memories of a far-distant past, when all was otherwise. They are not 'made-up', but have undergone their sea-changes in the course of time, and in the course of being told and retold hundreds of times.

Let us read them, then, with the background which we have already considered. The descriptive picture-images of our own primordial past can be found within the various creatures and personalities of legend and myth. Understanding the fable, and trusting the fabled, brings modern reverence to the 'memory preservers', and an enrichment to our own inner imaginative soul life.

The Celtic Tradition

A female divinity called Domnu seems to have signified the abyss or the deep sea. She and her son-King, Indech, ruled over a divine family called Domnu's gods. They were connected to the Fomors, an ancient race – more ancient than the gods. The name 'Fomor' is derived from two Gaelic words, meaning 'under sea'. They were the offspring of Chaos and Old Night and were often, as legend has it, huge and strangely shaped creatures. However, Elathan, one of their chiefs, was described in an old manuscript as having a magnificent presence, with golden hair, and clothing interwoven with threads of gold and a brooch of gold shining upon his breast. His son, Bress, means 'beautiful', and everything beautiful in Ireland was compared to him.

The Fomor god Balor, however, always kept one eye shut, as it rendered potent destructive magical powers which he had accidentally received from his father's sorcerers. The 'eye of Balor' became the expression, 'the evil eye'. Balor's Castle is the name of a curious cliff on Tory Island off the coast of Donegal, which was the Fomorian outpost on earth – their real home being in the depths of the sea.

Myths recall great battles, often utilising powers of magic and Druidic enchantment, between the Tuatha De Danaan, the gods of the Gaels (or the gods of Light) – whose home was at Tara – and the Fomors, the gods of the Iberians (or gods of Darkness).

The three main personages of the Fomorians – Balor, Bress and Elathan – carry individual characteristics, each very different from the other; the noble, fair sun-like quality; the beautiful; and the ugly, destructive aspect. In a way, the three together embody traits which are found in every human being at some level or other, and which can also be found at different stages of evolution. The Fomors, in their dwelling place deep beneath the sea, seem to be one of the original primordial

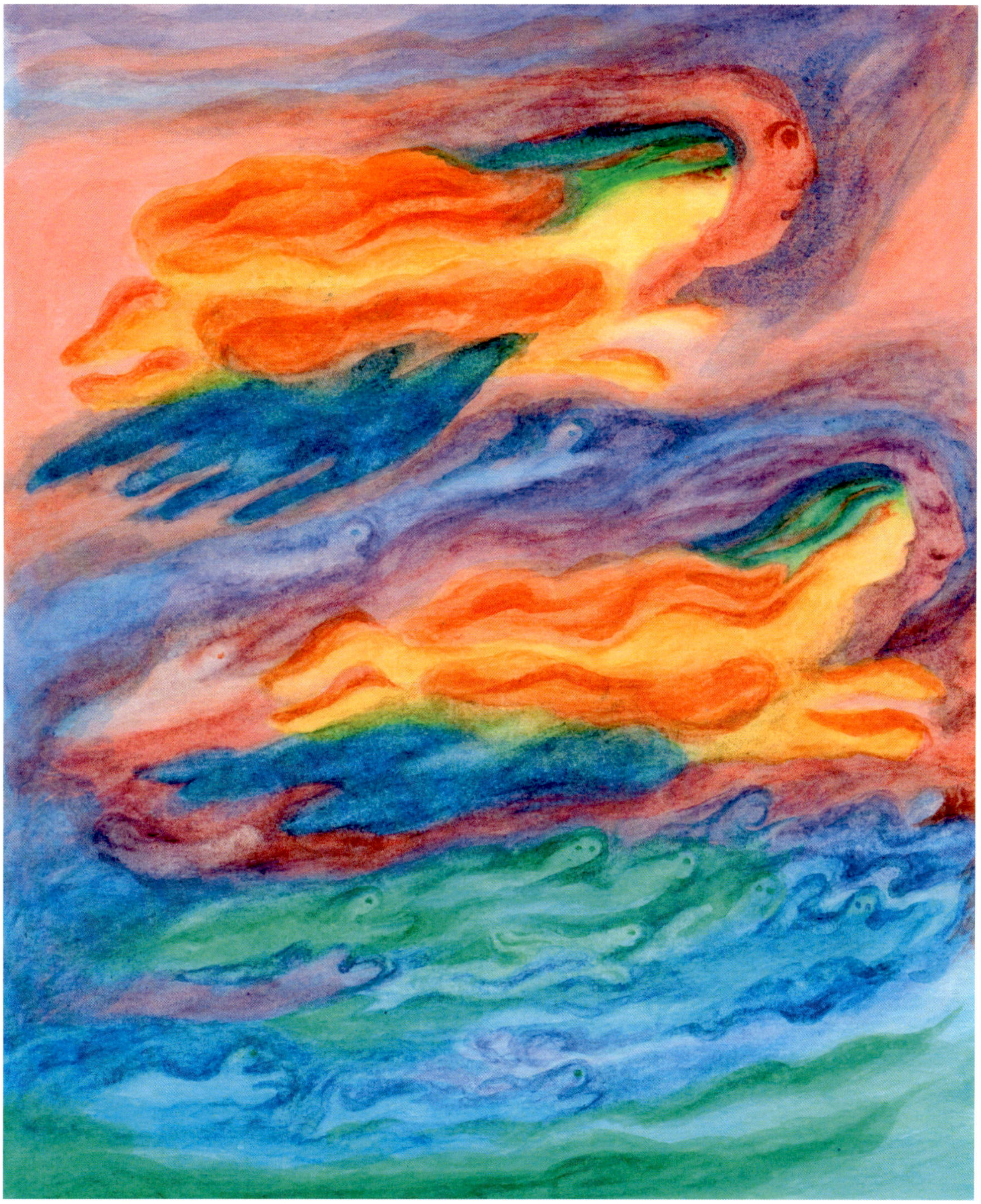

17. 'Creatures of the Sea' by the author

inhabitants of Ireland, existing there already before the arrival of the gods – or the race of higher beings – the Tuatha De Danaan, who according to some legends came to Ireland from the sky. Eventually, in the great battle known as the 'Battle of Moytura the Northern', the Fomors were driven headlong back into their country beneath the sea. An ancient manuscript states that: 'More Fomors were killed than there are stars in the sky, grains of sand on the seashore, snowflakes in winter, drops of dew upon the meadow in springtime, hailstones during a storm, blades of grass trodden under horses' feet, or Manannan son of Lir's white horses, the waves of the sea when a tempest breaks.'*

Eastern Mythology

In Buddhist and Hindu belief – from both a religious and a folklore tradition – the Naga are a species of supernatural half-human, half-snake creatures that, when they became too numerous on earth, were banished to the underworld by the god Brahma. In the underworld they live in regal style in magnificent palaces, under the rulership of their King, Mucalinda, spreading their hoods to provide shade for the gods and guarding over a great hoard of treasure.

Nagas, whose name in Sanskrit means 'serpent', are variously described as having many heads or else having the upper body of a human, with a long serpent's tail. Sometimes they have a miraculous jewel embedded in their head. They are closely associated with water, and are called upon to bring relief in times of drought. The Nagas are held in deep respect and reverence, and many noble Indian families claim descent from them. Generally, however, they leave mortals alone except when the latter have angered the gods, in which case they can use their poisonous bite to deadly effect.

Hindu mythology holds that the second member of the Hindu triad, Vishnu, has the role of being a protector, preserver and restorer. In the intervals (or great cosmic 'rests', referred to as pralaya), Vishnu sleeps on the cosmic waters, lying on the snake Sesha, whose seven heads spread out like a fan to make a canopy for him. This state of cosmic rest brings about the unfolding of a new universe, a new cycle of creation, into which Vishnu descends. One such descent is known as the Avatar (the descent) of the Fish, Matsya:

> One day when the wise Manu was making his ablutions he found in the hollow of his hand a tiny little fish, which pleaded for its life. Manu put it into a jar, but the next day it had grown so much larger that he had to carry it to a lake. Soon, the lake was too small. 'Throw me into the sea', called the fish 'and I shall be more comfortable'. Then he warned Manu of a coming deluge. He sent him a large ship with orders to load it with two of every living creature and the seeds of every plant, and then to board the ship himself. Manu carried out these

* Quoted from Charles Squire, *Celtic Myths and Legends*, Chapter Nine: 'The War with the Giants'.

orders just as the ocean began to swell and to submerge everything. Nothing was to be seen but Vishnu in the form of a huge one-horned fish with golden scales. Manu moored his ship to the horn of the fish, using the large snake Vasuki as a rope. Thus mankind, the animals and plants were saved from destruction from the mighty flood.*

Greek Mythology

The oldest water divinity was Pontus, who Gaia produced from herself at the beginning of time. He was without form, existing as the water of life itself.

Oceanus, a Titan born of Uranus and Gaia, was an immense river which formed a liquid girdle around the universe, containing the essence of all creation. Uniting with his sister, Tethys, he created three thousand Oceanids and three thousand rivers, and through his divine elemental force contributed to the formation of the world.

Nereus, a Greek god of the sea, was the sea-god before Poseidon. He was the son of Pontus (Sea) and Gaia (Earth). The hero Heracles had to hold on to him through a series of miraculous shape changes. In order to obtain the golden apples of the Hesperides, Heracles surprised Nereus and obtained from him the location of the sacred garden, which lay in the west on the slopes of Mount Atlas. The daughters of Nereus ('the old man of the sea') were sea-nymphs. They are sometimes depicted in paintings reclining on the backs of sea-horses. With the Tritons, they are the attendants of Neptune (Poseidon) and his wife Amphitrite (herself a Nereid), and play round them in the waves. Other nereids were Thetis and Galatea, the mother of Achilles.

Babylonian Mythology

The ancient Babylonians had references to sea-maidens, or Nereids. Their sea-god, Ea-Oannes, had power over the spirits, demons and creatures of the deep. Great giants of the sea are referred to in an ancient chant:

> Seven are they, seven are they
> In the ocean deep seven are they,
> Battening in heaven seven are they,
> Bred in the depths of ocean...
> Of the seven, the first is the south wind,
> The second a dragon with mouth agape...†

Tiamat the primordial sea-goddess gave birth to enormous serpents, dragons, tempest-monsters, scorpion-men, rams, hurricanes and fish-men. These were her creations in her rage against Ea, who had seized – through magical incantations – the god of the primordial ocean, Apsu, and the tumult of the waves, Mummu.

---

* Quoted from *New Larousse Encyclopaedia of Mythology*, Chapter: 'Indian Mythology'.

† Quoted from, *The Devils and Evil Spirits of Babylonia* by R. Campbell Thompson.

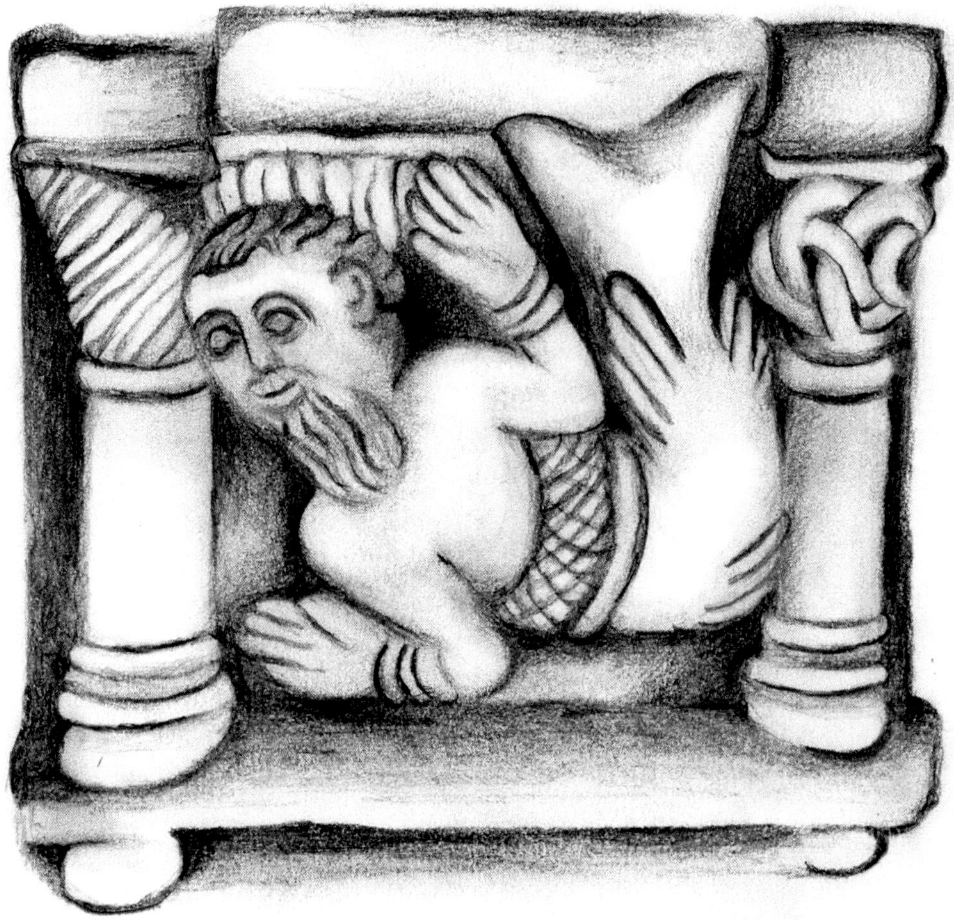

A. 'Merman. Romanesque relief from the Abbey of Alspach. Museum D'unterlinden, Colmar, France

Aztec Mythology

In the Aztec mythology, Chalchiuhtlicue was a water goddess and the symbol of youthful beauty. Quetzalcoatl drove Tlaloc, her husband, from the sky, and placed Chalchiuhtlicue there instead. But she caused such floods that only those who turned themselves into fish survived. Chalchiuhtlicue was portrayed as a river, from which grew a prickly pear laden with fruit.

Mermaids and Mermen

The folklore surrounding mermaids and mermen seems to capture and romanticise a sea-creature that is half human from the waist up and half fish from the waist down. These tales of sea-dwelling creatures are common in ancient mythologies throughout the world, and are surprisingly consistent in their descriptions. Mermaids are usually described as being beautiful women from the waist up, with long flowing golden hair, and having the lower body of a fish. Although mortal, they live much longer than humans. They inhabit a magnificent world under the ocean, together with their male counterparts, mermen. However, they frequently come up to the surface of the water to sit upon rocks, combing their long golden flowing hair, sometimes holding a mirror, and singing enchanting songs. So beautiful are their songs and their appearance that they are able to lure sailors and their vessels towards them, usually with tragic consequences. To see a mermaid on a voyage was considered to be an omen of a shipwreck or other misfortune. In some traditions, they are eager to drag mortals, especially the young men who are most susceptible to their charms, under the sea with them, where they keep their souls trapped in cages or under an enchantment.

Early Celtic tales tell of monstrous mermaids (the Fomors, referred to in 'The Celtic Tradition' section above), but in later folklore they developed into kindlier creatures, even offering advice to humans.

They are often accredited with the ability to grant three wishes, and in many folktales mortals succeed in catching a mermaid and demanding these wishes. Like most magical creatures however, although the mermaids are obliged to fulfil the wishes, they contrive to trick their captors by changing the outcomes. Since they cannot move on land, they are powerless if caught out by a rapidly receding tide – this was said to be one way of stranding a mermaid on shore. Another way was to entangle her in a fishing net. Some traditions hold that a mermaid could not survive long on land; others tell of mermaids who came ashore in human shape, or who married human males and lived on land for many years.

Common to all these stories is their deep longing to return to the sea. So great is this yearning that they are often able to persuade their husband or lover to return with them.

Mermaid legends have developed in different ways in different countries, although as we have seen, all share similar descriptions of their appearances and behaviour. Looking at them in more detail gives a fascinating collective picture. Keeping in mind the descriptions of humanity's earlier stage of evolution enables a deeper reading of the mermaid legends through which we can discern certain aspects of truth. In this sense, folklore becomes the long handed-down tradition of what was, at one time, the condition or state of our own very ancient existence.

A Tradition from Brittany

The Bretons believe in mermaids, naming them Morgan, meaning sea-woman, and Morvec'h, meaning sea-daughters. Anyone who ventures too close to the edge of the water can be drawn down to the bottom of the sea by them, to their palaces of gold and crystal, which also lie beneath the water of lakes and pools. Morgans sing and comb their golden hair. In one of the ballads we read '"Fisherman, hast thou seen the mermaid combing her hair, yellow as gold, by the noontide sun, at the edge of the water?" I have seen the fair mermaid. I have also heard her singing. Her songs were plaintive as the waves.'*

British Legends

Near the Lizard, a man named Lutey helped a stranded mermaid back into the water. In gratitude she gave him her comb and said that he and his descendants would be

---

* From *The World Guide to Gnomes, Fairies, Elves and Other Little People, Compendium of International Fairy Folklore* by Thomas Keightly.

able to break witches' spells and control demons. Nine years later, however, she came back for him and drew him under the waves. In the 1840s, the folklorist Robert Hunt was told that several Cornish families claimed to have uncanny powers because of being descended from a mermaid or a merman. On the other hand, a mermaid was reputed to have ruined Padstow harbour with sandbars, because someone there had shot at her.

At Marden (Herefordshire), a church bell once fell into a deep pool in a river where a mermaid seized it. At Child's Ercall (Shropshire) a mermaid from a pool was about to give some men 'a lump of gold, as big as a man's head, very near'. When one of the men swore in amazement, she shrieked and vanished beneath the water.*

A Cornish man, Matthew Trewhella, had a most wonderful singing voice. His tuneful singing in the parish church of Zennor in Cornwall lured a mermaid out of the sea. He fell in love with her, and in turn was lured beneath the waves. According to local legend, his singing could be heard coming from the sea for many years after.

The mermaids from the Welsh border do not live in the sea, but in rivers and lakes. In Ireland, some traditional tales hold that they are considered to be early female pagans who were banished from the land by St Patrick, along with snakes and sea-serpents. On the coast, they are referred to as Merrow, or Moruach, meaning 'sea-maid'. Some legends tell of marriages formed by mortals with these sea-maids, from which some families in the south claim to be descended, owing to their children having webbed hands or feet. Merrows are usually seen shortly before storms break out.

According also to Scottish legend, the Selkie, or Silkie, married mortals and became the source of famous Scottish families. The evidence of these origins was said to be the webbed hands or feet of the children.

Selkies had various attributes: they were considered to be fallen angels disguised in the form of seals, who could put on the guise of a human. Selkies would remove their skins and go undetected among mortals, but if a mortal found the sealskin of a female Selkie, he could force her to live with him as his wife. Various tales record how humans ensnared Selkie wives who bore them human children before finally retrieving their sealskins and returning to the sea. It was said that if anyone killed a Selkie, and allowed the blood to drip into the sea, their own ship would be lost in a storm.

An alternative name for seals in Scots Gaelic is Cuilein Mairi, which can be translated on several levels. Literally, it can read as 'Mary's Whelps', that is, young creatures or offspring (a cub or even a young man). Cuilein can also be read as a verb meaning 'to bring forth' or 'to originate'. Perhaps the word Mairi can find its origins in Mare, the sea. However we regard this term, it has its source in a pictorial sense for the sea-creature as having a divine origin, as a creation of Mary, or of having its origins as a young creature on the sea.

From Italy

In the reign of Roger, King of Sicily, a young man happened to be bathing in the sea late one evening. He perceived that something was following him in the water. Supposing it

* Quoted in *Dictionary of English Folklore* by J. Simpson and S. Roud.

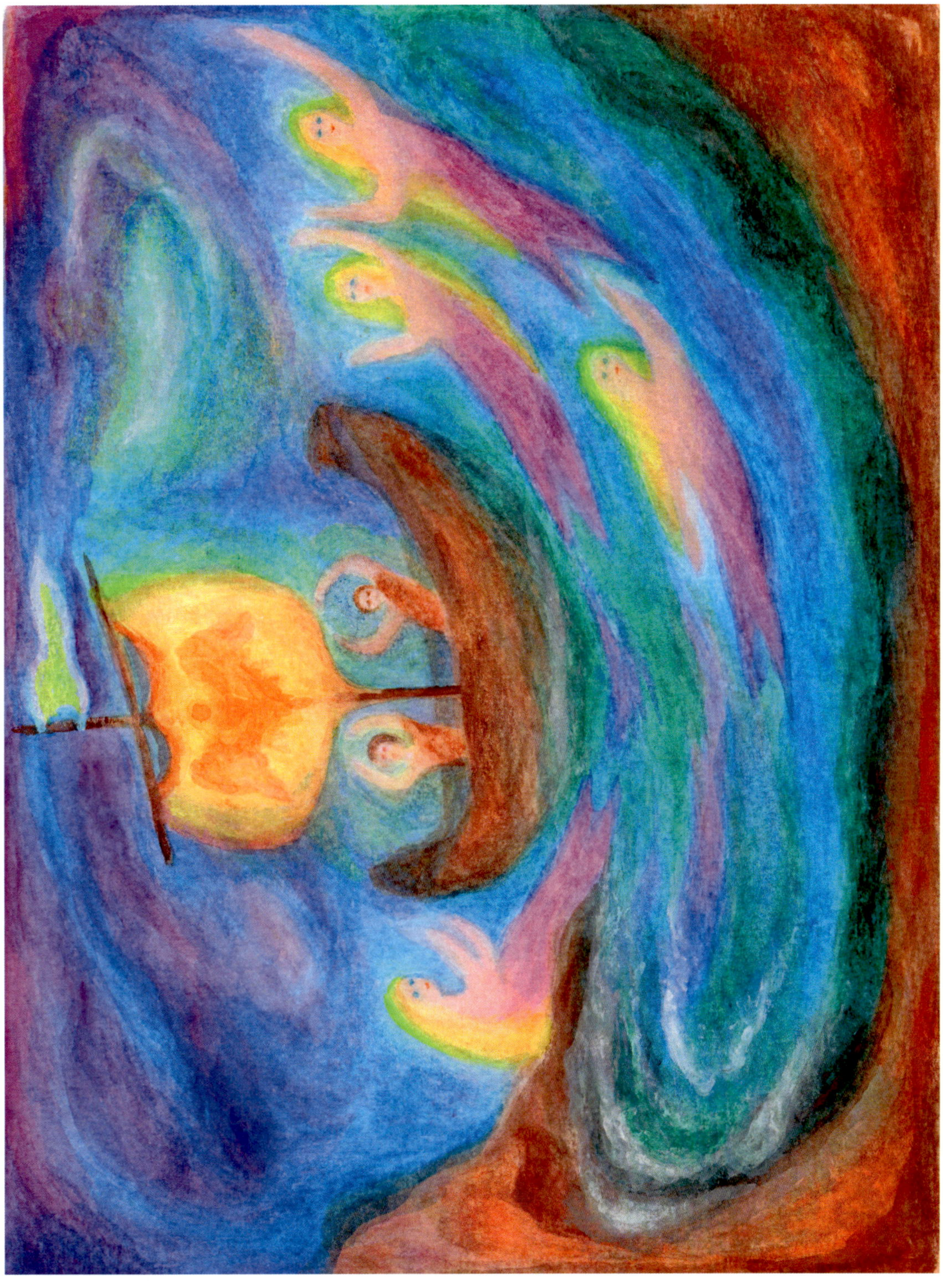

18. 'The Mermaids' Song' by the author

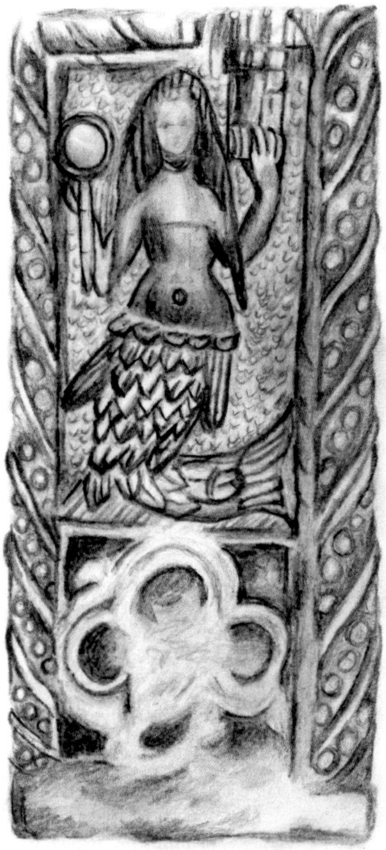

B. Medieval bench end. Carved wood. St Nonnan's Church, Cornwall.

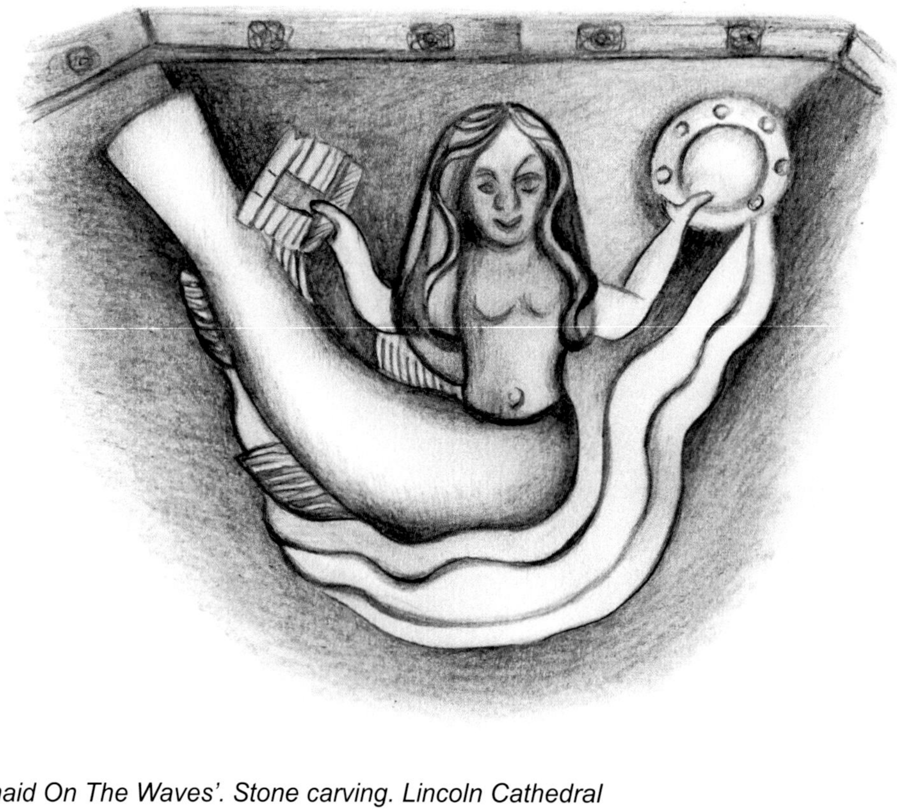

C. 'Mermaid On The Waves'. Stone carving. Lincoln Cathedral

to be one of his companions, he caught it by the hair and dragged it to shore. Finding it to be a young maiden of great beauty, he threw his cloak over her and carried her home. Eventually, she bore him a son. There was one thing, however, which greatly grieved him. That was the observation that so beautiful a form should be dumb – for he had never heard her speak. One day he was reproached by one of his companions, who said that it was a spectre and not a real woman that he had at home. Being both angry and terrified, he urged her with vehemence to tell him who or what she was, threatening, if she did not do so, to kill their child before her eyes. The maiden replied, saying he had lost a good wife by forcing her to speak, then instantly vanished, leaving her son behind. A few years later, as the boy was playing on the seashore with his companions, the spirit-maiden, his mother, dragged him into the sea where he was drowned.*

Finno-Ugric Mythology

An evil water-spirit named Nakk lived in the deepest depths of the water. Nakk could appear in many different shapes, both human and animal, though the Estonians usually imagined him as a grey old man who swallowed everything in the water that came his way. Sometimes he seated himself on the shore to watch people or to bewitch them with his songs, which forced people and animals to dance until they fell into the sea and were drowned. The female counterpart of Nakk was Nakineiu, Nakk's maid, a beautiful girl who sat on the surface of the water, on a rock near the shore, or in the shadow of a tree growing near the river, combing her long golden hair. Sometimes she appeared naked, having a half-human and half-fish body. Like her male counterpart, she too sang.

Slavonic Traditions

Here, the Rusalki were water maidens, who varied in their appearance and characteristics. Along the Danube and Dnieper rivers, they were charming and alluring, with skin like moonlight, and clothed in floating delicate mist. They sang beautiful songs, captivating passers-by with their sweet voices. They were both aquatic and sylvan, that is, dwelling in both water and air.

When the sun had not yet entered 'the path of summer', the Rusalki, who were also considered to be the souls of drowned maidens, would remain in the dark, cold waters. But when these waters were warmed by the rays of the life-giving sun, the Rusalki would enter into the green trees, which were believed to be the dwelling places of the deceased. There they would sit, combing the streaming water from their long flowing hair.

In Northern Russian regions, Rusalki were considered to be malevolent and less attractive, with wan cadaverous complexions and tangled uncombed hair. They would seize their victims for drowning, and treat them cruelly.

In Slavonic Mythology, the Vodyanoi was a water being – the name derived from *voda*, meaning water. They lived in lakes, pools, streams, rivers and under mill-wheels. Some had a human face, but had paws instead of hands, large toes and feet, and sometimes long horns and a tail. Others resembled humans of vast stature and were covered with grass and moss, having large red eyes and long noses.

---

* From *The World Guide to Gnomes, Fairies, Elves and Other Little People*, op. cit.

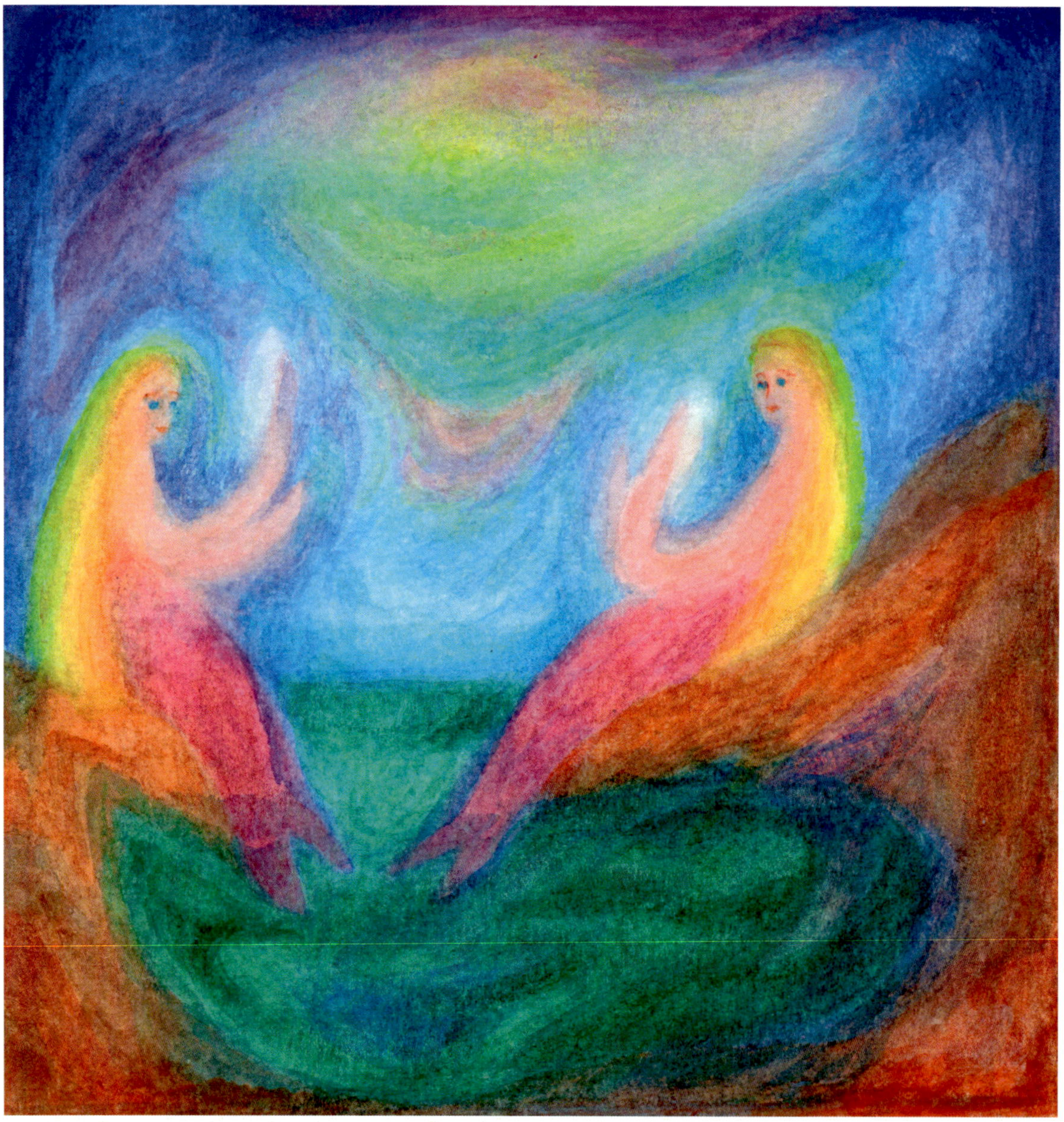

19. 'Mermaids II' by the author

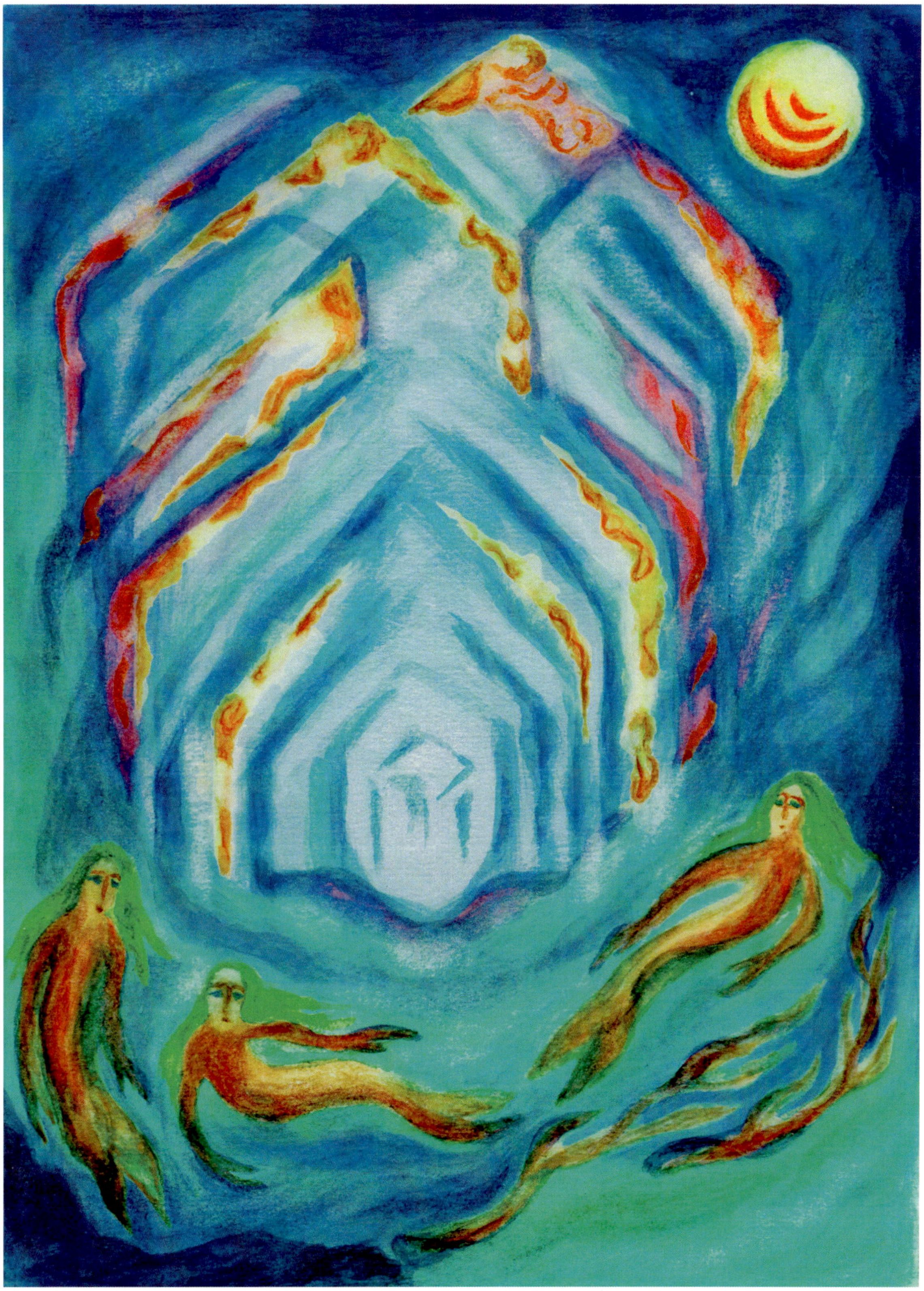

20. *'The Crystal Palace' by the author*

Often the Vodyanoi could resemble an old man with green hair and beard, which became white when the moon was waning. They could also appear in the guise of a naked woman, sitting in the water on the roots of a tree, combing the streaming water from their hair. The Vodyanoi were also seen having the appearance of a huge fish covered with moss, or sometimes seen similar in form to a winged tree-trunk flying along the surface of the water. The Vodyanoi were immortal, but they grew younger or older with the phases of the moon. They did not like human beings, and the drowned who fell into their deep and watery kingdom became their slaves. They lived in a crystal palace, ornamented with gold and silver from sunken boats, and lighted with a magic stone which shone more brightly than the sun.

During the day they would descend and rest in the depths of their palace. At night they would rise to the waters' surface, striking it with their paws and making a noise which could be heard at a great distance.*

Malay culture

A Malay poem relates how, once upon a time, in the city of Indrapura, there was a wealthy merchant who was very prosperous but had no children. One day, as he and his wife were walking by a river, they found a baby girl, as fair as an angel. They brought the child to their home and called her Bidasari. The merchant caused a golden fish to be made and into this fish he transferred the soul of Bidasari. He then put the golden fish into a golden casket full of water, and hid it in a pond in his garden.

In time the girl grew to be a beautiful woman. Now, the King of Indrapura had a fair young queen who lived in fear that her husband would take a second wife. Hearing of the beauty of Bidasari, the queen resolved to get her out of the way. She lured her to the palace and tried to kill her, but Bidasari could not die because her soul was not in her. At last she said to the queen: 'If you wish me to die you must find the golden casket which is in the pond in my father's garden'. So the golden casket was found and opened, and there was the golden fish in the water inside it. The maiden said: 'My soul is in that fish. In the morning you must take the fish out of the water, and in the evening put it back in the water. Do not let the fish lie about, but bind it around your neck, and I shall soon die'.

This the queen did, and the lovely Bidasari fell into a swoon, but in the evening, when the golden fish was put back into the casket, she came to herself again. Seeing that she had the girl in her power, the queen sent her home to her adopted parents, who, realising the ordeal she had been through, decided to take her far from the city. They had a house built in a lonely desolate place where Bidasari lived, undergoing the changes which were brought about by the vicissitudes of the golden fish, which was her soul.

One day the king was out hunting and, coming to the house where Bidasari lived, found her lying unconscious. Smitten by her beauty, he tried in vain to awaken her. He came later the following day, towards evening, and when darkness fell she came to herself and told the king of her circumstances. The king returned in haste to the palace,

* Source: *The Larousse Encyclopaedia*.

took the golden fish from the queen and put it into water. Bidasari revived and the king took her to be his wife.*

The Pacific region

Myths which originate in the Pacific region also recall an under-sea existence. Hina, the beautiful and completely unashamed wife of Maui (the favourite trickster hero of Polynesia), was originally the wife of the great Monster Eel, Te Tuna. They lived together in their dwelling place beneath the sea. The day came when Hina thought she had been there long enough as the place was intensely cold, and besides, she had had enough of Te Tuna. Telling her husband that she would be away for some days and nights, searching for food, she set out on a journey, coming first to the land of Tane. There she cried out that she was the first to come without shame to seek a lover upon the shores of Raro-nuku, the Land-below, and of Raro-via-i-o, the Land-of-penetrating-waters. However, the Tane clan called out to her that she should continue her journey, for they would not unite with the wife of Te Tuna lest they be slain by him.

She continued on her way, receiving similar responses from the other clansmen, until eventually she reached the home of the wonder-worker Maui, whose mother, Hua-hega, encouraged her son to take Hina for himself. So Maui-tikitiki-a-Taraga (Wonder-worker, the Tumid, begotten of the Ascending Shadow) took Hina for his wife.

Te Tuna, beset by chattering gossip, was eventually roused to anger. He set a huge wave – with storms, lightning and thunder – against Maui, who quelled the great surge of water which receded until the seabed was laid bare and Te Tuna and his creatures were stranded. Maui set upon three of the creature-companions, but spared Te Tuna who came to Maui's house, where they lived all together in harmony.

Eventually, however, Te Tuna challenged Maui to a duel in which each would go completely 'into the body' of the other. When that was over, Te Tuna would kill Maui and reclaim his woman, and return with her to his own home beneath the sea. Maui agreed, and the Giant Eel began chanting an incantation:

> The Orea-eel swings and sways
> The Orea-eel balances his head lower and lower,
> He is a mighty monster who has come hither
> across the ocean from his distant isle.
> The monster contracts, becoming smaller and smaller.
> It is I, Te Tuna, who now enter your body!

---

* See *The Golden Bough, a Study in Magic and Religion*, by James Fraser. Chapter: 'The External Soul in Folk-Tales'.

With this, Te Tuna disappeared completely into Maui's body, and only after a long, long while did he come out again. Maui had not been disturbed in the least, and then took his turn, chanting his own spell first:

> The Orea-eel swings and sways,
> The Orea balances his head lower and lower
> A small man stands erect upon the land
> The man contracts – becoming smaller and smaller.
> It is I, Maui, who now enter O Te Tuna, into your body!

Maui, the Wonder-worker, disappeared completely into Te Tuna's body, and at once all the sinews of the Great Eel were rent apart so that he died. Maui cut off Te Tuna's head, carrying it away to give to his grandfather, but his mother persuaded him to bury it near their house. They continued with their daily lives until, sometime later, Maui saw with amazement that a new shoot had sprung up from the sand where Te Tuna's head had been buried. Hua-hega told him that the plant was a kind of coconut known as the 'husk of the sea-green colour from the region of the gods', as it had arisen from the depths of the sea to reveal to them the colour of its own land. It would provide them with rich gifts – inside the fruit would be food to eat, and drinking bowls would be made from its husks. The great Monster Eel's head had become transformed.*

---

* This legend can be read in full in *The Masks of God: Primitive Mythology*, by Joseph Campbell, chapter titled 'The Ritual Love-Death'.

Chapter Two
A Cabinet of Curiosities

The following illustrations show various aspects of the awareness of relationships existing between fish – or sea-creatures – and humans. These images have their origins in various cultures and from different times. They are fascinatingly curious and each could lead into its own chapter of research. However, they are gathered here together to give a glimpse into that 'which has suffered a sea-change, into something rich and strange', including gods and goddesses, idols, sacred objects as well as somewhat grotesque creatures, the altogether inexplicable and exotic.

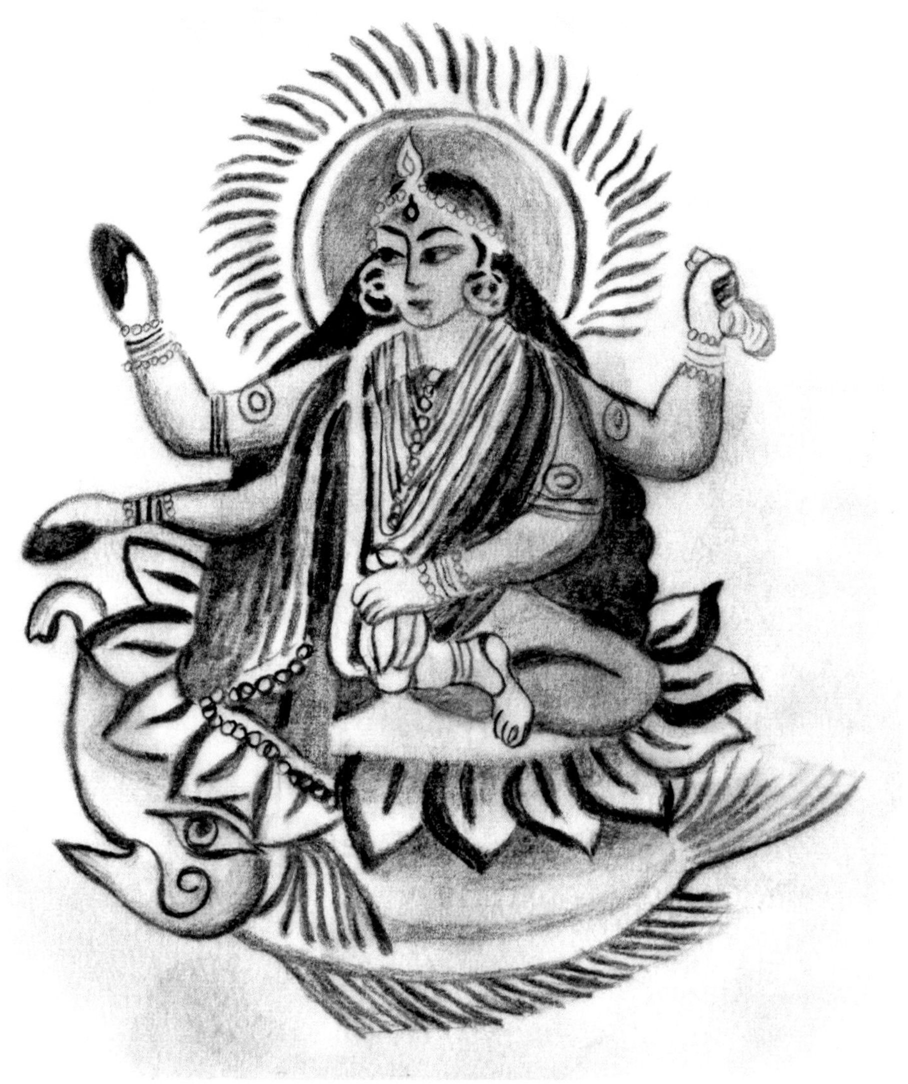

D. Shiva seated upon a lotus flower, supported by a Ganesh/fish form. Shiva, together with Vishnu and Brahma, form the Trimurti, the triad of great gods. Ascribed to the Indus Valley culture, 3,000–1,500 BC. A god of creation, time and destruction, depicted here sustaining the world through meditation, rather than by the usually depicted cosmic dance. Painting, 1890. (Victoria and Albert Museum, London.)

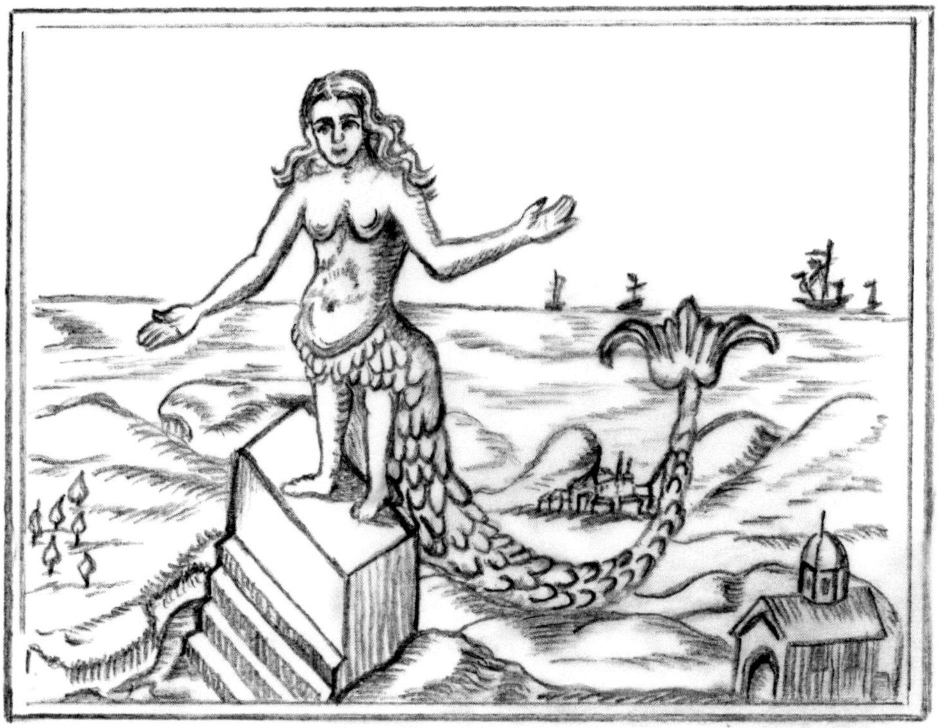

E. Dagon. From Oedipus Aegyptiacus *by Athanasius Kircher (Rome 1652). Dagon, 'The Great Fish', an idol with the body of a human being and the tail of a fish, worshipped by the Philistines at Ashdod (1 Samuel 5, verses 1-7). (Source:* The Three Books of Occult Philosophy *Book III.)*

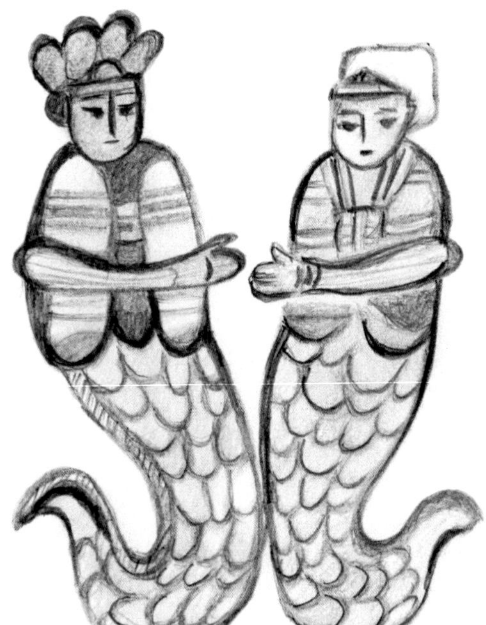

F. Fu Hsi, the mythical sovereign whose reign is ascribed to the years 2953–2838 BC, and his sister-wife-successor, Nü Gua. Both had the body of a serpent (or, seen here, as fish-like), he a more ox-like head (or animal-like), and she more human, endowed with divine wisdom. They were sometimes described as the only two humans in existence, and were placed at the foot of the K'un-lun Mountains. (Original carved relief image from History of Mythology.*)*

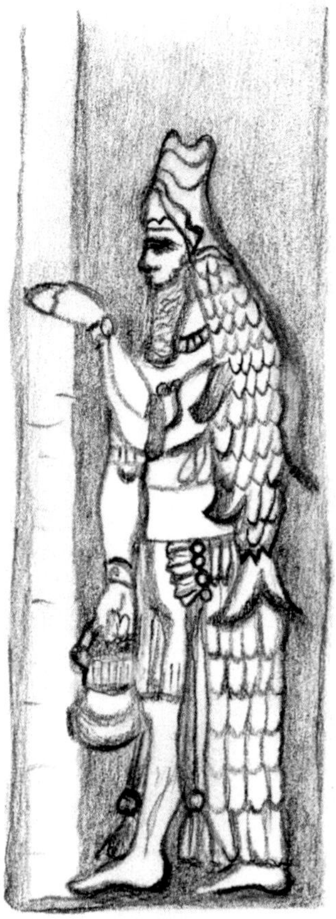

G. A Sumerian Priest in ritual costume. Legends held that a fish-like god had descended, with a human head beneath the fish's head, and feet like a man beneath the fish's tail. Divine fish-men appeared periodically, coming ashore from the Erythrean Sea, which bordered on Babylonia. Ancient texts describe the craft of the Nefilim as celestial boats appearing from the sea, from which 'fish-men' emerged. (Source: The Twelfth Planet, Zecharia Sitchin.)

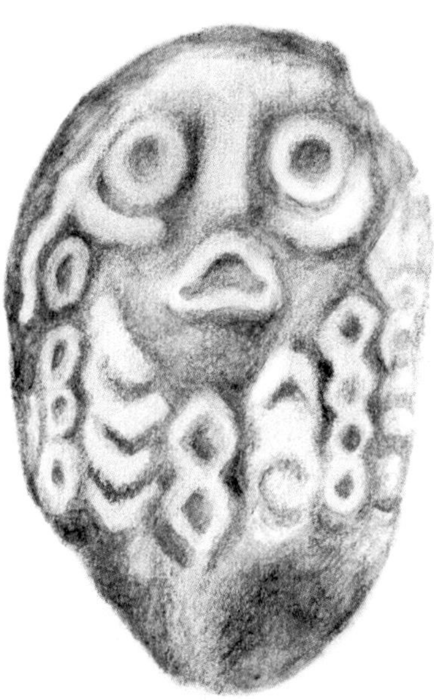

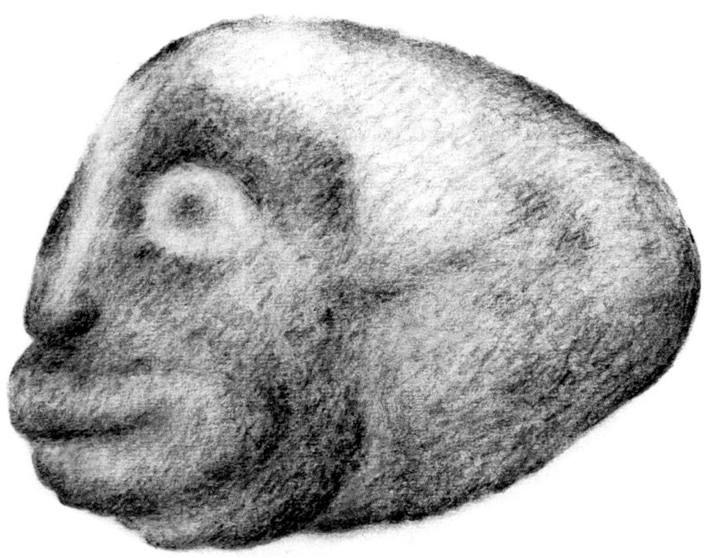

H. I. Stone carvings of human/fish figures, C.6400 BC from Lepenski Vir, a site of hunters and fishermen of the Old Stone Age, excavated on the banks of the Danube River, Slovenia, in 1965. (Source: After the Ice.)

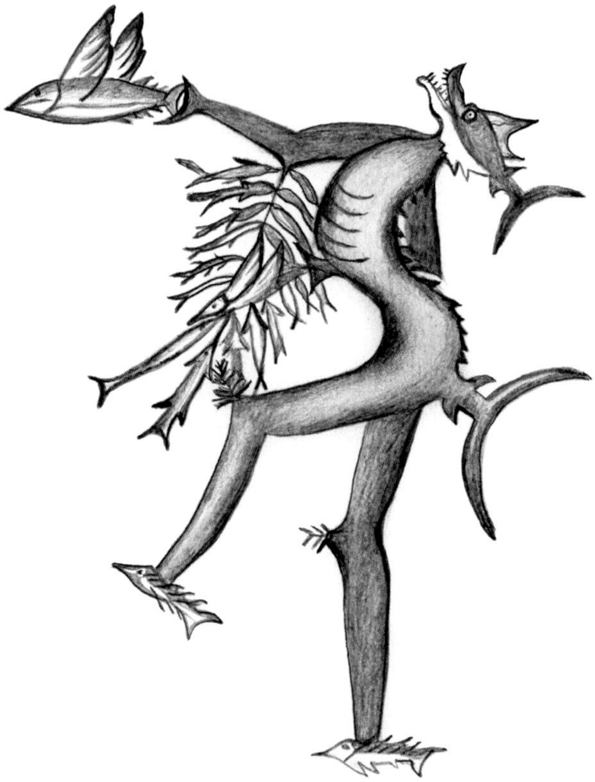

J. Native drawing of a sea spirit. San Cristoval, Solomon Islands. (Source: Mythology of All Races, *Vol. 9.)*

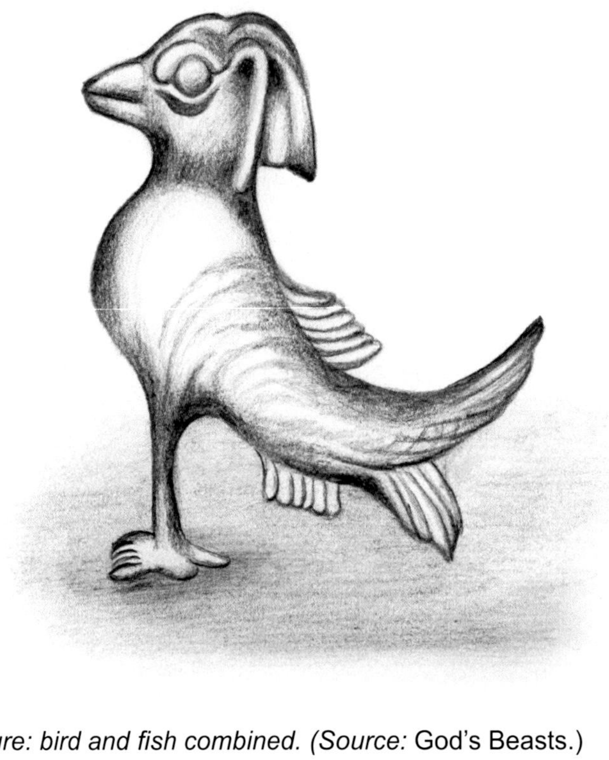

K. A composite creature: bird and fish combined. (Source: God's Beasts.)

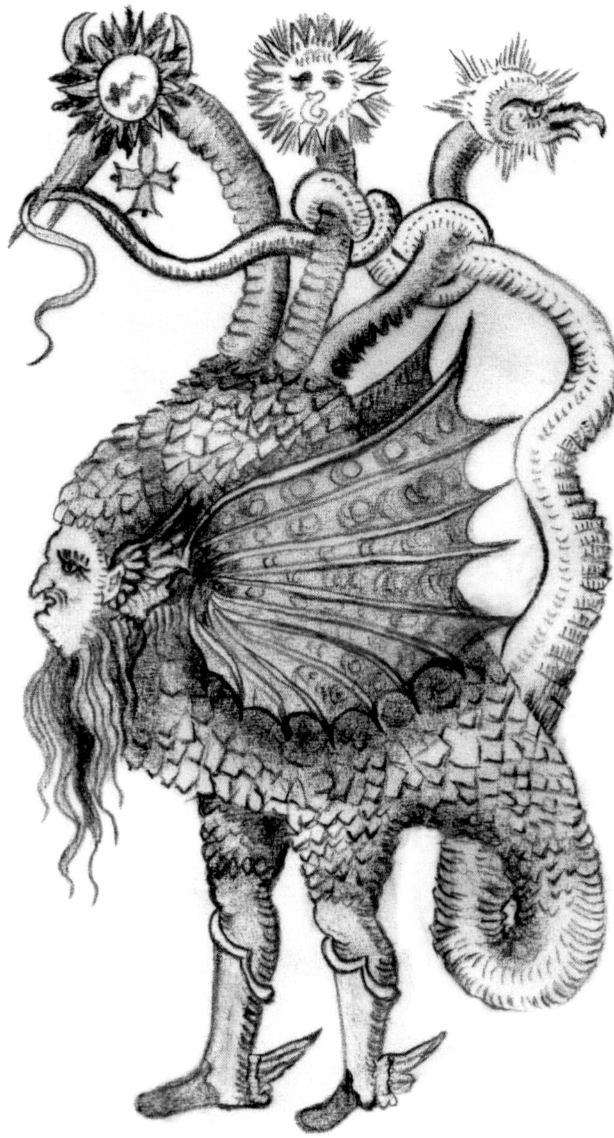

L. This alchemical illustration shows a composite being of human-animal-reptile-fish. On the three protruding tentacles are symbols representing saturn, sun and moon. (Source: A Divine Magic.)

Chapter Three
The Sphinx

'The secret powers, since old Atlantean days, when they would commence hold with mankind, have often taken form of bird or beast – bull, dragon, eagle. Thus, in guise we know, they bridged the vastness twixt ourselves and them'.
– 'The Song of the Salmon God' by W.P. Ryan

Surrounded by dry desert sand and baked by the Egyptian sun, the enigmatic Sphinx seems a long way removed from our creature swimming beneath the water. However, a certain kinship can be detected, in that both bear the head of a human being and hind-quarters – which in one case are aquatic, and in the other case are similar to a land-based animal, or perhaps even to several animals. The Sphinx combines animal and human features. It actually has a fourfold nature – the head human; its fore-paws are those of a lion; the body is both lion and bull-like; and, in some cases, it also has wings. Sphinxes are found in Egypt, Assyria and Greece – all represent something mysterious; a mystery which can be understood when we look back into humanity's past, into the time of Atlantis.

> Think about this recollection of ancient Atlantean consciousness, symbolically placed before man in Egyptian times. The Egyptian priest wanted to say to his people, 'In Atlantean times your souls, when awake, beheld the human form in animal shape; during the night, however, a beautiful human head grew out of it'. This memory, represented sculpturally, is the Sphinx. These forms can only be understood in this way … they are not contrived, they are realities.*

This human being in ancient Atlantean times appeared, when seen physically by day, to be almost similar to an animal, with a strongly receding forehead and protruding teeth. By night, however, when asleep and able to see clairvoyantly, the Atlantean would appear in an etheric form with a human head shaped even more beautifully than in our present time.

Four great influences from the spiritual worlds poured into the Atlantean constitution. These took the archetypal forms of lion-human, bull-human, eagle-human and human. Gradually, these physical types became harmonised through the work of the developing human ego. The fourfold Sphinx is the embodied memory – represented so magnificently in stone – of the Egyptian initiate-priests' perception of the cosmic formative forces, which were active in shaping the human form. The priest, able to see clairvoyantly into the past, knew of these great shaping forces. The Sphinx reminded the Egyptian that, again and again, the human being individualised out of the spiritual realms into the physical world. The form he possessed, and the features which were his

* R. Steiner, August 14 April 1908, Stuttgart, GA105. Quoted in *The Language of Colour in the First Goetheanum* by Hilde Raske, Chapter: 'The Egyptian Epoch'.

own as an ancient Egyptian, were vastly different from those of his previous Atlantean incarnation, and would eventually be changed again in the distant future.

The riddle of the Sphinx conceals human evolution. We can recall that these four particular animal and human forms are also recorded in the Bible, in the Book of Revelation, Chapter Four:

> And round the throne, on each side of the throne, are four living creatures, full of eyes in front and behind: the first living creature like a lion, the second living creature like an ox, the third living creature with the face of a man, and the fourth living creature like a flying eagle. And the four living creatures, each of them with six wings, are full of eyes all around and within, and day and night they never cease to sing, 'Holy, holy, holy is the Lord God Almighty who was and is and is to come!'*

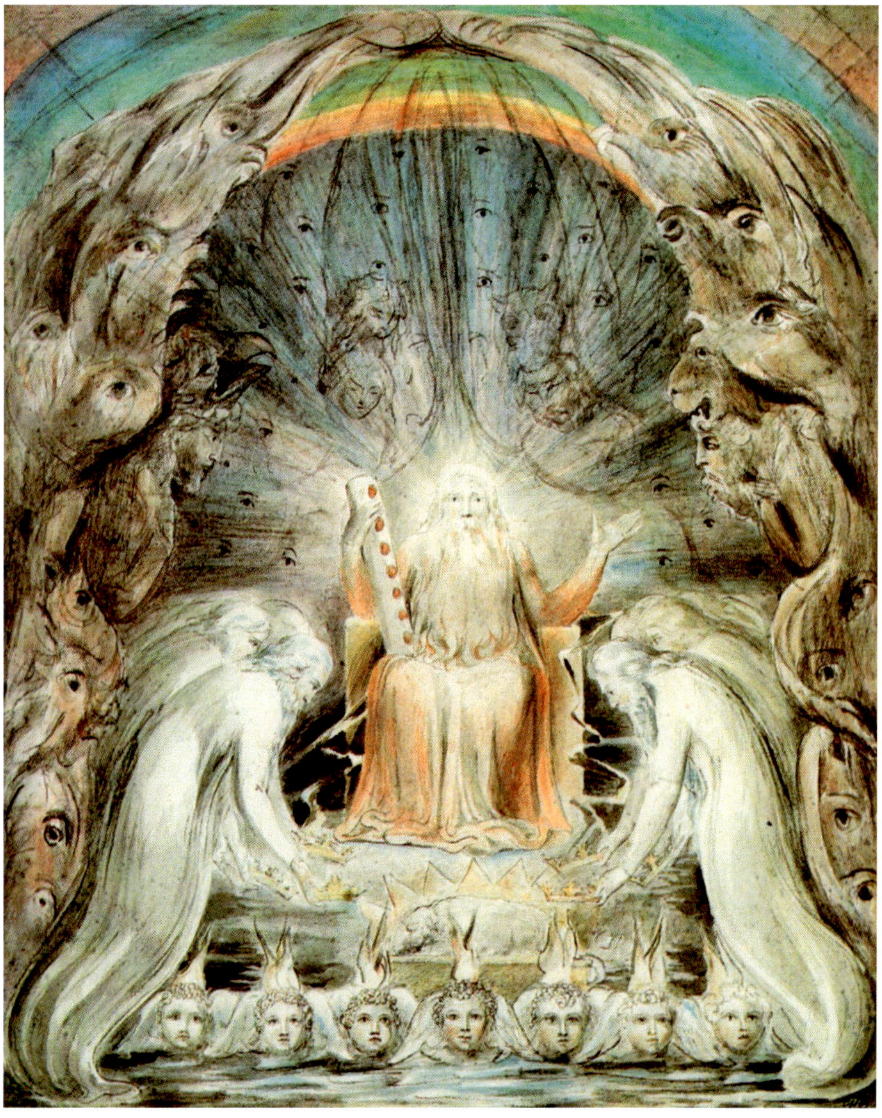

21. 'The Four and Twenty Elders Casting their Crowns before the Divine Throne' by William Blake.

---

* Revised standard version of the Bible, Revelation 4: 6-9. See also *The Apocalypse of St John* by R. Steiner, Lecture 6, Nuremburg, 23 June 1908 (GA 104).

PART SIX

Chapter One

The Symbol of the Fish in Christianity

'Jesus then took the loaves, spoke the words of blessing over them and shared them among those who were seated, he did the same with the fish – all received as much as they wanted.'
– Gospel of St John, Chapter 6

A sign frequently used by the early Christians was a simple depiction of a fish, which denoted a Christian person or a Christian place of worship. They could be found in the early catacombs, on rings, gemstones and coins, and carved onto gravestones. Later, they were included in Celtic manuscripts and carved in stone or wood in many churches.

In church tradition it became a symbol of Christ originating with the acrostic, in which the first letters of the five Greek words for 'Jesus Christ, Son of God, Saviour' form the word ΙΧΘΥΣ when put together, meaning fish or ICHTHUS (or sometimes ICHTHYS); in Greek: *Iesous Christos Theou Huios Soter*.

Tertullian described baptism: 'But we small fishes, named after our great ICHTHUS, Jesus Christ, are born in water and only by remaining in water can we live.' As well as being a reference to baptism, the water could also symbolise the living water of life which was related to the watery life-substance in early evolution. We find this in the Bible in the Book of Genesis in the following words: 'The Spirit of the Elohim brooded over the waters.'

Rudolf Steiner indicates that the Elohim were embodied in the whole cosmos: 'In the elements of air and water lived their bodily part, in the element of warmth their spiritual part.'*

In the early years of the Church, the fish was sometimes a symbol of the Eucharist – its imagery arising from the miracles of the feeding of the five thousand and the four thousand with fishes and loaves of bread, as recorded in the New Testament of the Bible.†

The Vesica is a name meaning fish and is given to the radiant light – or the aura – shining around Christ's figure, which was seen as an oval or fish-shape. An almond-shaped interpretation of this form is called a mandorla.

In his lectures published as *Universe, Earth and Man*, Rudolf Steiner gives us an esoteric understanding of the fish: 'This symbol did not appear suddenly. Long before

* *Genesis*, Lecture II.

† The Gospel of St Matthew, Chapter 14, and the Gospel of St Mark, Chapter 8.

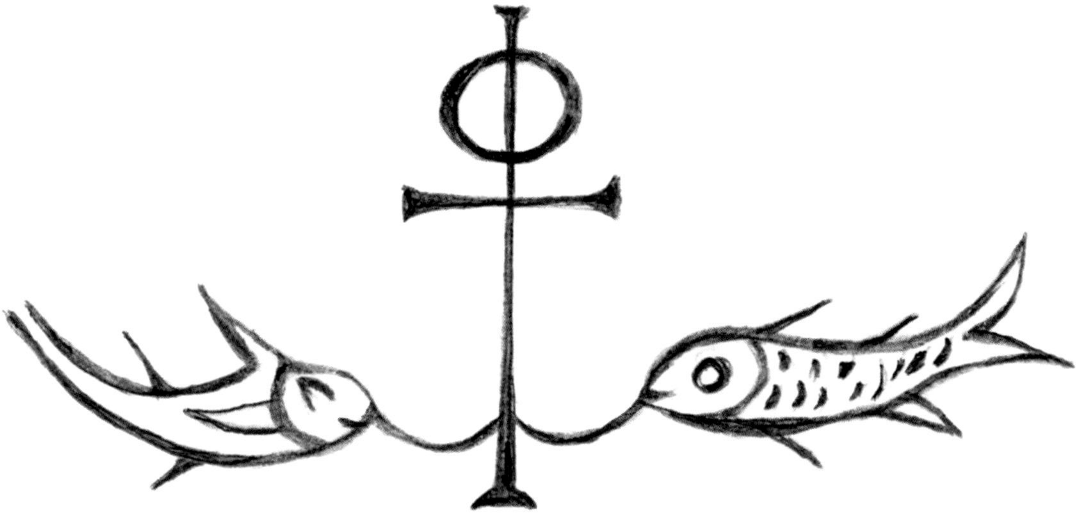

M. The Anchor Cross with Fishes.

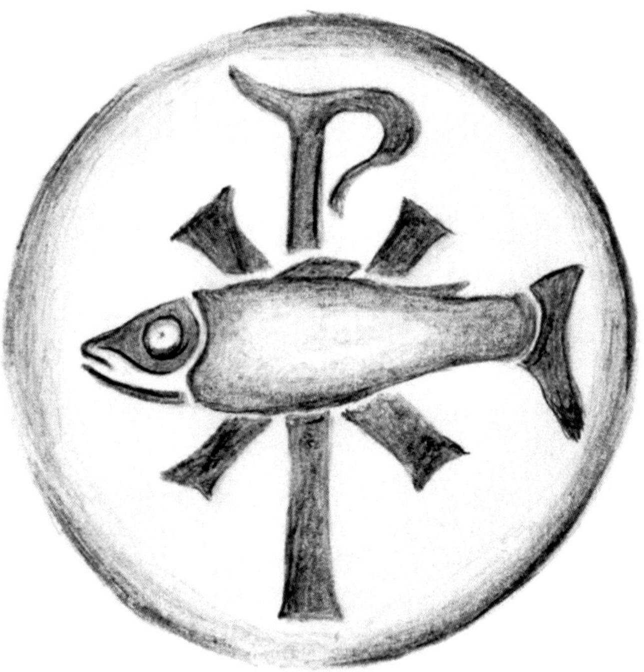

N. Fish with PX Monogram. (Both taken from: Christian Symbols, Ancient and Modern. H. Child and D. Colles.)

the coming of Christ, the prophets of the Messiah had directed their pupils [neophytes], to His coming, and everywhere, back to the Druidic Mysteries, the fish symbol played its part.'*

We can ask, what did the fish signify? The initiates had the duty to remind their pupils of humanity's ancient home on the sun, during the sun phase of evolution. The symbol they used for this was the symbol of the fish. This is why it appears in the catacombs as a true symbol connected with the evolution of humanity: 'The disciples of the early centuries, seeing the fish symbol everywhere, received the words of the initiates which rang in their ears with deep emotion, for inwardly it led them to the inward holiness of the story of Palestine, and at the same time led them forth cosmically into the mighty evolutionary phases of the earth… the symbol of the fish is a token of that which was cultivated within the Mysteries.'†

Here we can ask, what was the content of the Mysteries? What did the symbol of the fish represent in this context? Rudolf Steiner describes this as follows:

> As humanity evolved gradually, the animal forms were thrust aside. Human beings had only a very fine etheric form at the time when the earth and sun were still united. When these separated, certain animal forms were separated out from the human form and these remained behind at the stage in evolution which corresponds to the time when the sun was still within the earth. From these, entirely different forms have naturally arisen in the course of time, for we are concerned here with a very long after-development. Were we to select a characteristic form which is still to be found today, and which in some way be compared with those which remained behind when the earth was separated from the sun, we can select the form of the fish. This is the form which remained over when the earth became more reliant on its own resources; it is that which still has within it the last echo of the sun-forces.
>
> The beings who represented the first material-spiritual construction of the human form (which was only to the extent of the etheric and astral bodies, invisible to our sight), at the time of the sun's departure, have undergone manifold changes. But in fishes is preserved that which reminds us of our separation from the sun; reminds us that at one time we belonged to the sun.‡

After the departure of the sun, there came a change in the constitution of the early human beings, namely an experience vaguely similar to our present-day waking and sleeping life, with the reversal of consciousness: during the 'day' we were more in a dreaming condition; during the 'night' we were dimly conscious of a spiritual world around us.

---

* *Universe, Earth and Man*, Chapter VII.

† Ibid., Chapter VII.

‡ Ibid., Chapter VII.

The Fish

The sun did not yet penetrate through the earth's dense atmosphere, but we nevertheless received divinely beneficial influences from spiritual forces emanating from it. Later – eons later – there was an event in world-evolution when an exalted sun-being entered into the stream of evolution in a direct manner, bestowing spiritual forces into humanity. This was the Christ being. Inward spiritual power streamed into humanity; radiant light entered into world evolution 2,000 years ago, to enlighten the hearts and minds of humanity, who were becoming increasingly ensnared in materialism. Just as once we received outer physical sun-forces, now light and spiritual forces entered into our inner nature, and continue to do so.

The fish became a reminder of humanity's time of innocence. When we see peacefully swimming fishes, surrounded, supported and sustained by the water, we sense deeply – beneath our everyday consciousness – a quiet serenity, a sense of peace within our soul. This, at a deep inner level, reminds us of our former innocence when we had as yet no ego, but were carried by higher spirits of world evolution, within whose being we 'swam' – supported and carried by their divine presence.

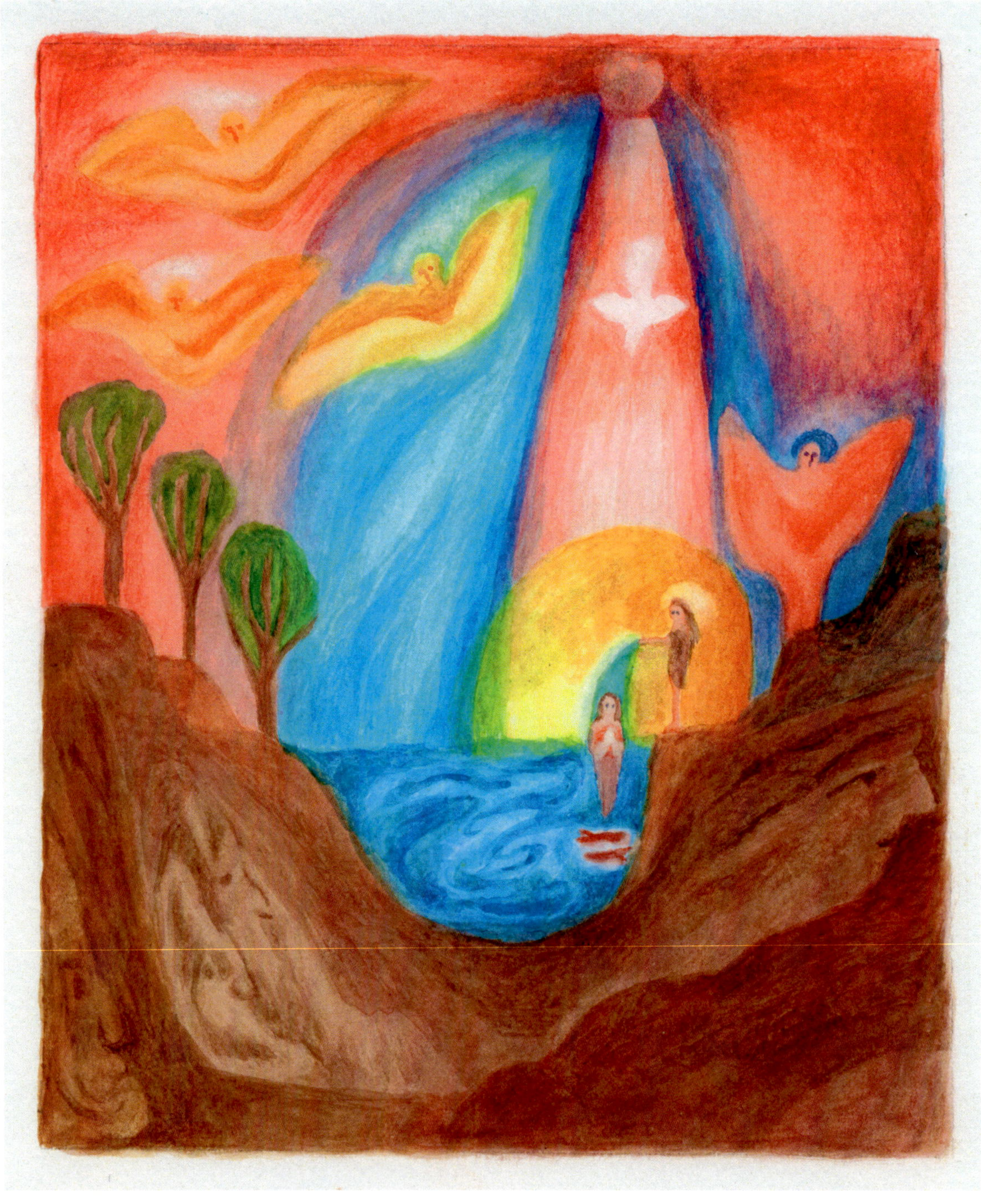

22. 'The Baptism' with the colour of Pisces (rose-pink), by the Author

Chapter Two
The Zodiac

And did those feet in ancient times
Walk upon England's mountains green?
And was the Holy Lamb of God
In England's pleasant pastures seen?
– William Blake

A further aspect of the Fish as symbol can be considered in relationship to the zodiacal signs, the Fishes being the pictorial image for the sign of Pisces. Each sign of the zodiac is related to an aspect of our human body, with Pisces being connected to the feet.

From each region of the zodiac and from the planets, forces stream from the cosmos and build up our constitution when we are still in the spiritual worlds, creating our bodies before birth. At one time – we could say at the dawn of time – our whole being extended across the universe. We really did touch the stars! Spiritual beings within the starry realms worked within particular constellations, streaming forces into the cosmic human being that created the individual aspects of what would become, aeons later, our earthly form. What previously existed as the primal human being on ancient Saturn, sun and moon was not uniformly shaped; though each was a true human being, it was only later that all systems flowed together in one human form.* The Archai received the human being over from the Exusiai, for whom the human being was still a cosmic thought-form. The Archai transformed this thought-form into an etheric form of such a nature that it already possessed forces capable of bringing forth human beings' physical form. The development of this form, in the sign of Pisces, brought about a wholly new trend in evolution: human beings detached themselves as microcosms from a unified cosmos. Two centres thus came into being. The human being had to set out as a microcosm in order to understand the macrocosm.

The 'Mysterium of Two', cosmically regarded, thus becomes a 'Piscean Mysterium'. There are always two fish in this sign. We see this duo in the paired organs within our form: hands and feet, our eyes and ears.

The cosmic moment when the sun stood in the sign of Pisces, marked the end of a creative round and the beginning of earth's evolution. The sun separated from the earth, with the moon remaining as a watery earth-moon planet.

When a further zodiacal round of creation had run its course, and the sun stood once more in Pisces, paradisal human beings lost their home there and began the earthly pilgrimage. This occurred at the end of the Lemurian epoch.†

* See R. Steiner's *The Michael Mystery*, Chapters 16–17.

† See Erasmy, Hedwig, *Cosmic and Human Evolution*, chapter titled: 'The Realm of Pisces – N'.

Soul Calendar Verses for the Spring, The time of Pisces, 19 February – 23 March

23 February – 1 March
There will arise out of the great-world-womb
The joy of growth, quickening the sense of life.
May it find my sense of thought
Supported by the strength of Gods
Who strengthen me in my inner life.

2–8 March
In light, that out of worldwide heights
Would powerfully flow into the soul,
Appears the certainty of cosmic thinking
To solve the soul's enigma,
And focusing its mighty rays
Awakens love in human hearts.

9–15 March
I feel the force of cosmic life:
So speaks my clarity of thought,
Recalling its own spirit growth
In dark world-nights
And toward the approaching cosmic day
It turns its inner rays of hope.

16-22 March
There speaks to the human ego
In mighty revelation
While it unfolds its life forces
The world-beings' urge to become:
In you I carry my life
From its enchanted bonds
And so attain my true goal.*

Although these verses are difficult to understand on first reading, reflecting on them can reveal subtle aspects of the cosmic and earthly worlds in relation to human consciousness. They express the relationships between the wider world of spiritual beings and the inner soul life of the human being for the Piscean time of the year.

* Translated by Ruth and Hans Pusch.

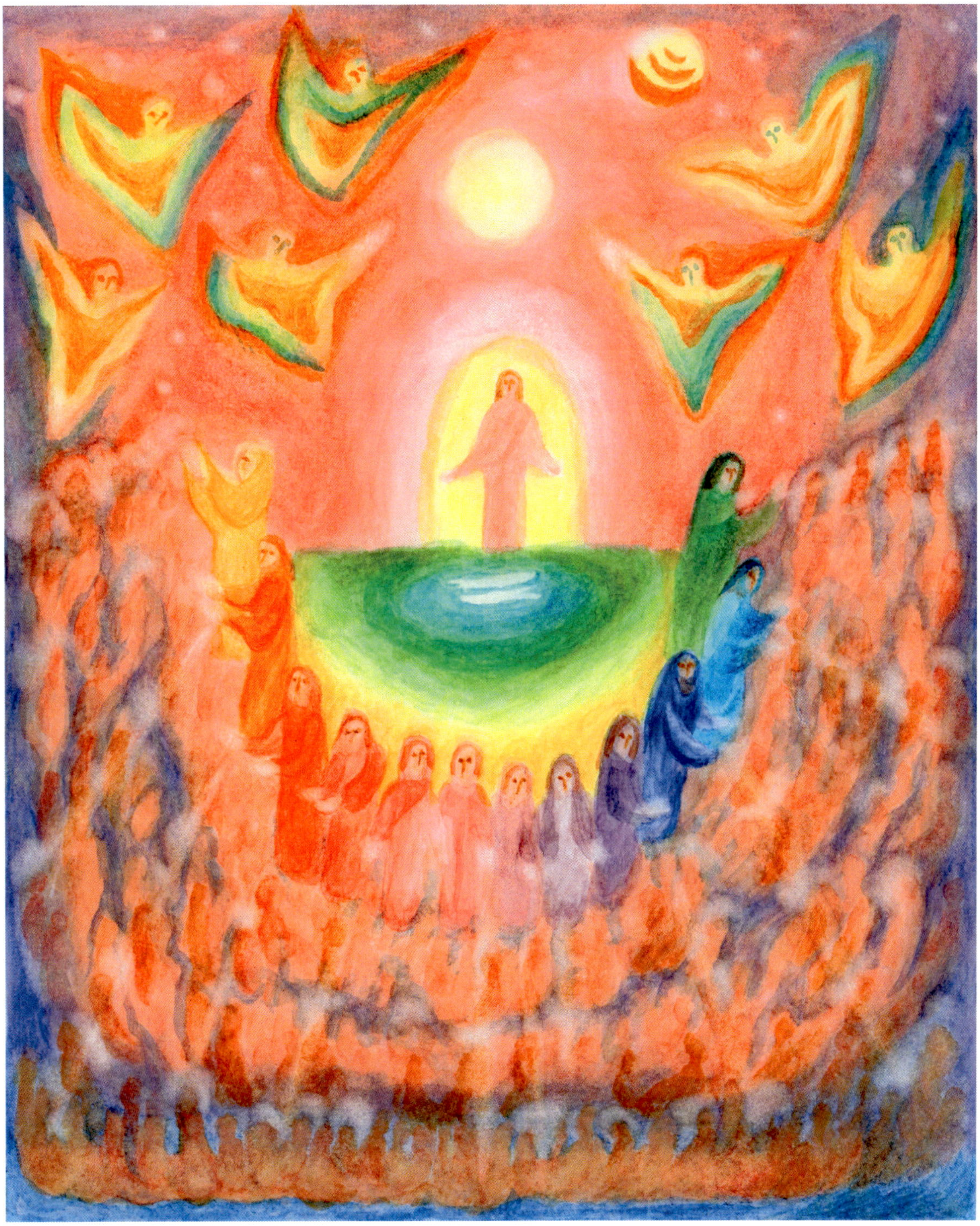

23. *'Feeding the Five Thousand' – the Miracle of the Loaves and Fishes, by the author.*

Chapter Three
The Evangelists

'From the midst of the fire came the likeness of four living creatures. They had the form of men but each had four faces and four wings... each had the face of a man in front, the face of a lion on the right side, the face of an ox on the left and the face of an eagle at the back... and they shone as burnished bronze... And when they went, I heard the noise of their wings, like the noise of great waters, as the voice of the Almighty...'

– Ezekiel, Chapter 1

The early Christians thought that the four Gospel writers had souls which were representative of entire groups of human beings, and that they were therefore not like ordinary human souls. A human group soul is born at the boundary between the physical and astral planes – that is, in an etheric state – at a certain time, and it transforms itself at a certain time. There are four main types, but there are countless intermediary stages also.*

The human group-soul or group-ego is formed by human beings' fourfold nature. The further back in time we go, the more human beings were divided into four human groups according to their etheric bodies. These four groups resembled the etheric bodies of the eagle, the lion, the bull and the human being. People used to think that different etheric groups had these imaginative animal forms, which were in reality a memory of the group souls that humanity had in ancient times.

Humanity had lived in soft, gelatinous, animal-like forms, that corresponded to their various group-soul natures, until the middle of the Atlantean epoch. Four distinct phases of development had taken place in the first four root-races of Atlantis, during which the water in the air was the bearer of humanity. The three later phases of Atlantis saw the development of an individuality in human consciousness, which began in the vicinity of present-day Ireland.†

The inspired writers of the Gospels were therefore attributed with the great etheric archetypes of these groups: Matthew with the winged human being; Mark with the winged lion; Luke with the winged bull; John with the winged Eagle.

'The inspired Gospels could give expression to the truth about Christianity only because they were written with the remnants of atavistically clairvoyant wisdom.'‡ This statement indicates the spiritual awareness that was still possible during Graeco-Roman times, and which enabled the Evangelists to compose the Gospels. It also gives the basis for early Christians being able to perceive the etheric imaginations.

We can find many artistic depictions of the Evangelists in Christian traditions with their corresponding winged beings.

---

* Rudolf Steiner, lecture of 27 December 1907 (Cologne).

† See Rudolf Steiner's *The Apocalypse of St John* (GA 104).

‡ Rudolf Steiner, *Three Streams in the Evolution of Mankind*, Lecture Three.

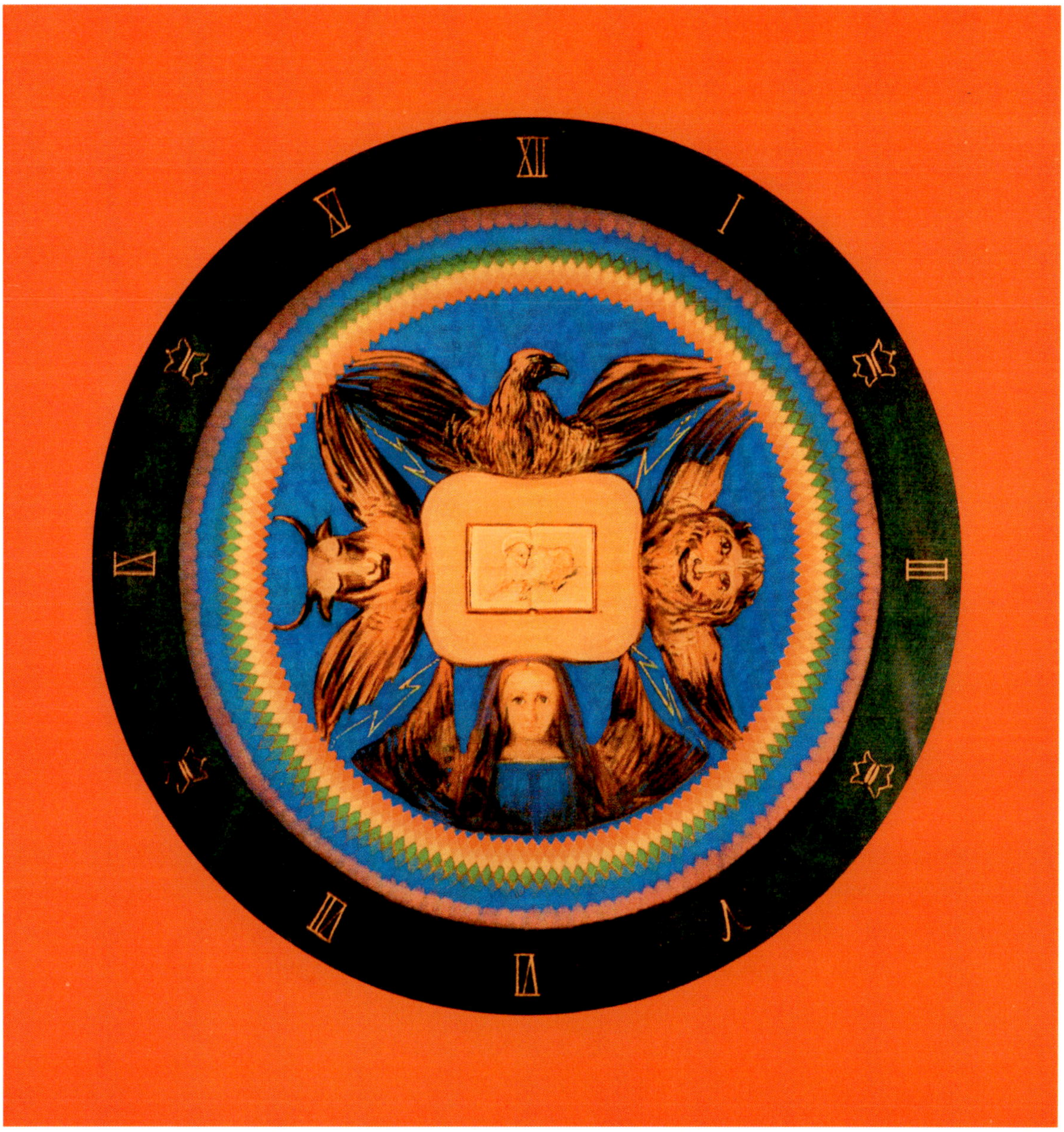

24. *'The Archetypal Animal and Man', from the Apocalyptic Seals painted by Clara Rettich.*

PART SEVEN

Chapter One
The Colours of the Motif

The first impressions of the Archetypal Human-Animal painting are those of strong colouring and strong contrasts. We see first of all a yellow and red creature swimming in a watery environment, with indigo fingers of algae, or plant-like shapes below it. The colours are intense; the forms are vigorous and strong. The orange head is seen in profile, having a humanly-shaped nose and a slightly opened mouth. It has an unusual red eye, which seems to be looking upwards, forwards and backwards all at the same time. Green 'hair' covers the head, with stripes of orange. It has a dark reddish-brown backbone. Golden yellow arms and feet extend from the front and back, and the hands have rudimentary fingers; each foot has an individual form. An undulating yellow wave or ripple goes through the red body. This is actually a rudimentary digestion canal.

The strange finger or hand-shaped indigo forms are based on primitive algae structures. They criss-cross over each other; some seem to be attached to the lower part of the red 'body'. The whole creature is suspended in surroundings that have a watery nature, and which are blue and cool red in colour.

In order to paint this image it is necessary to consider the sequence of colours, and how Rudolf Steiner was able to paint the motif from 'out of the colour'.

The Toned Page – An Approach to Painting

Rudolf Steiner suggested to painters that the background into which they would paint could be coloured with a pale wash of one colour. If this background colour was, say, a cool blue, then the whole 'direction' of the painting would be influenced by this blue. The forms and gestures of the colours would be influenced by blue – they would be 'moving' within a blue world, and would respond accordingly. He suggested that experiments could be made using different coloured backgrounds, and painting a colour into each one. So, for example, a yellow could be painted onto a white, a yellow, an orange, a red, a green, blue or violet-toned paper (the coloured backgrounds would be quite pale). The toned background-colour would create a particular colour environment into which the yellow would come. The task of the artist would be to identify so deeply and so intimately with the colour, that it would be possible to sense each response and to paint the yellow accordingly, giving the yellow a different form in each different situation.

The following questions could be asked: 'What does yellow do on a white paper?' What does yellow do on a green paper?' How does yellow feel on a blue paper?' 'How does yellow move on a violet paper?' And so on.

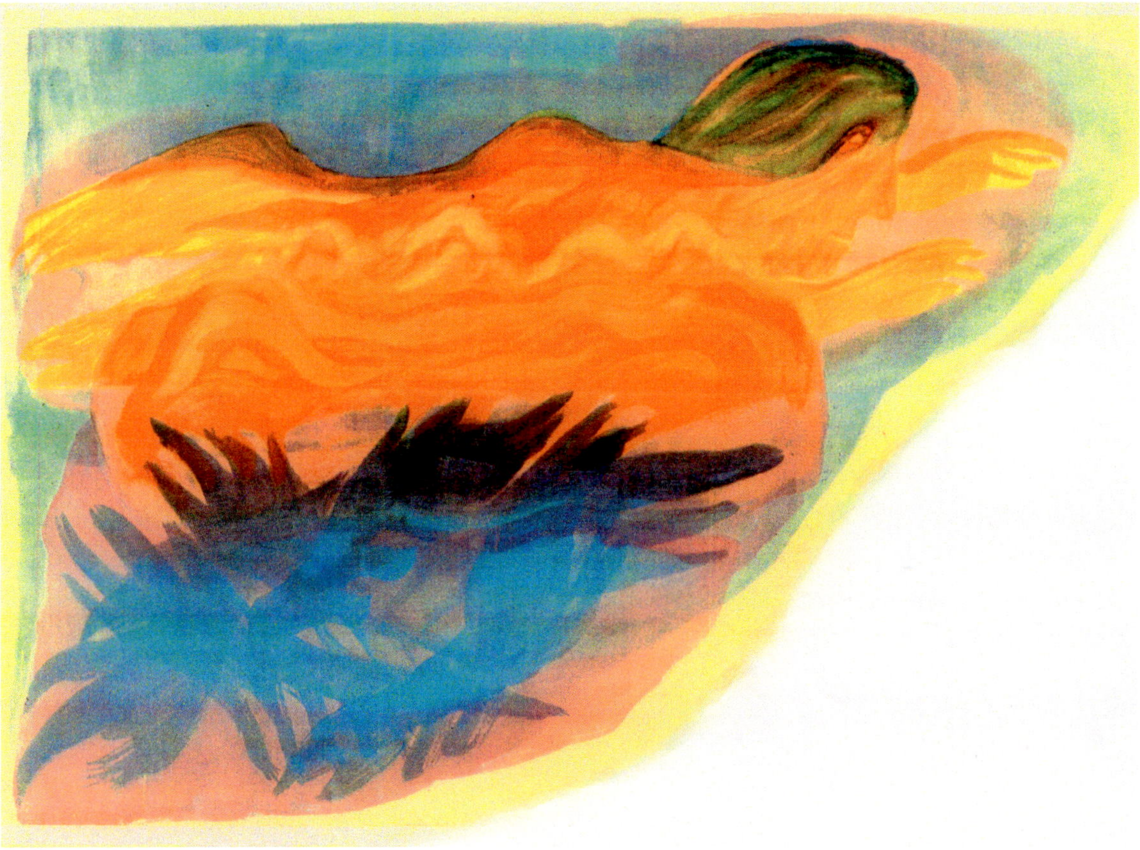

25. *'The Archetypal Human-Animal' by Rudolf Steiner.*

This method of working with colour brings the artist towards the nature of the colour itself – what the colour is seeking to do; how the colour wishes to express itself. Eventually it would become possible to sense accurate responses arising from the colours themselves, thus allowing forms, gestures and movements to develop from the interactions of the colours as they respond to the differing toned papers.

The archetypal 'human-animal' is surrounded by two different colours – a cool blue and a cool pinkish-red. Looking closely at the painting we can see a small area of cool red – without blue – between the 'feet' of the swimming creature. This could suggest that the background colour was cool red, and that blue was painted later. It is important, however, for an artist to make experiments and to try out various colour possibilities.

Colour Sequences and Colour Polarities in the Motif

It is possible to make different experiments with this motif in order to research the colour-responses. One sequence can be:

1. A toned crimson page.
2. Bringing a medium yellow onto the crimson page,
   or bringing a cool yellow
   or bringing a warm yellow.

Already, we have three possibilities, as the yellows have different qualities and will create different forms.

Another colour sequence would be to bring yellow onto a cool blue background. Again, experiments can be made with different yellows in order to gauge their reactions.

Following this, the painter can decide whether to strengthen the periphery, or to strengthen the centre. Blue or cool red can be painted in the surroundings; a deeper yellow or a warm red can be brought into the centre. A constant balancing is required between inner and outer, above and below. If the centre becomes too strong, then more blue or cool red is needed on the periphery; if the centre is too weak then it can be strengthened with orange, then a stronger warm red.

The warm yellow hands and feet extend the figure out into its surroundings. The head develops when one has the inner feeling that the colours need to gain a consciousness – that a focus is needed. Green or blue in the head-area brings calmness and steadiness, providing a quiet mood in contrast to the yellow, orange and red. The indigo below brings an activity which is cool and dark, contrasting with the light, warmer colours above. Here, unusually, the darker, cooler colours are as active as the lighter, warmer colours above them, which makes an opposition, or polarity, in the painting, bringing a forwards-thrusting movement to the swimming creature. The contrast between the strong blue and the equally strong vermilion also adds to the dynamic activity. This is further enhanced by surrounding the bright red-yellow creature with a contrasting blue, and by surrounding the deep-blue plant forms with a soft, cool red.

Some of the plant-forms are veiled with a more intense layer of cool red, creating dark mixed colours, which again brings about a contrast of light and dark in the painting, giving a sense of buoyancy or weightlessness to the swimming creature. By contrast, the darker colours seem to be denser and more solid than the lighter colours. Here we have a polarity of 'weight' in the darker colours and 'weightlessness' in the lighter colours. The density or solidity of the darker colours also makes the red (in the upper area) and the blue (in the lower area) appear to be brighter and more transparent. The red and the blue both gain a radiant quality through the contrasting darker and denser nature of the mixed colours.

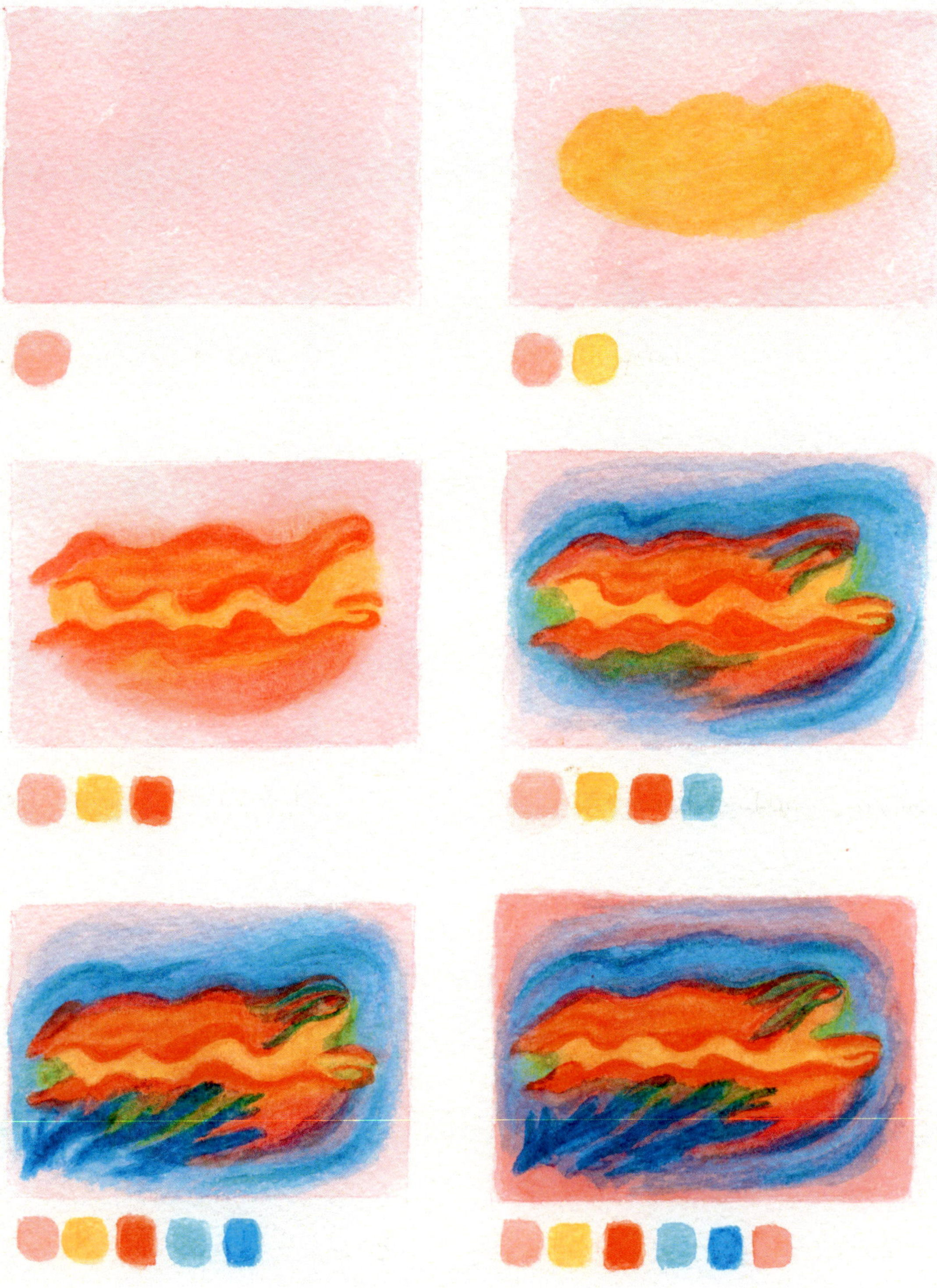

26-30. *Colour Sequences for Painting the Archetypal Human-Animal Motif, by the Author*

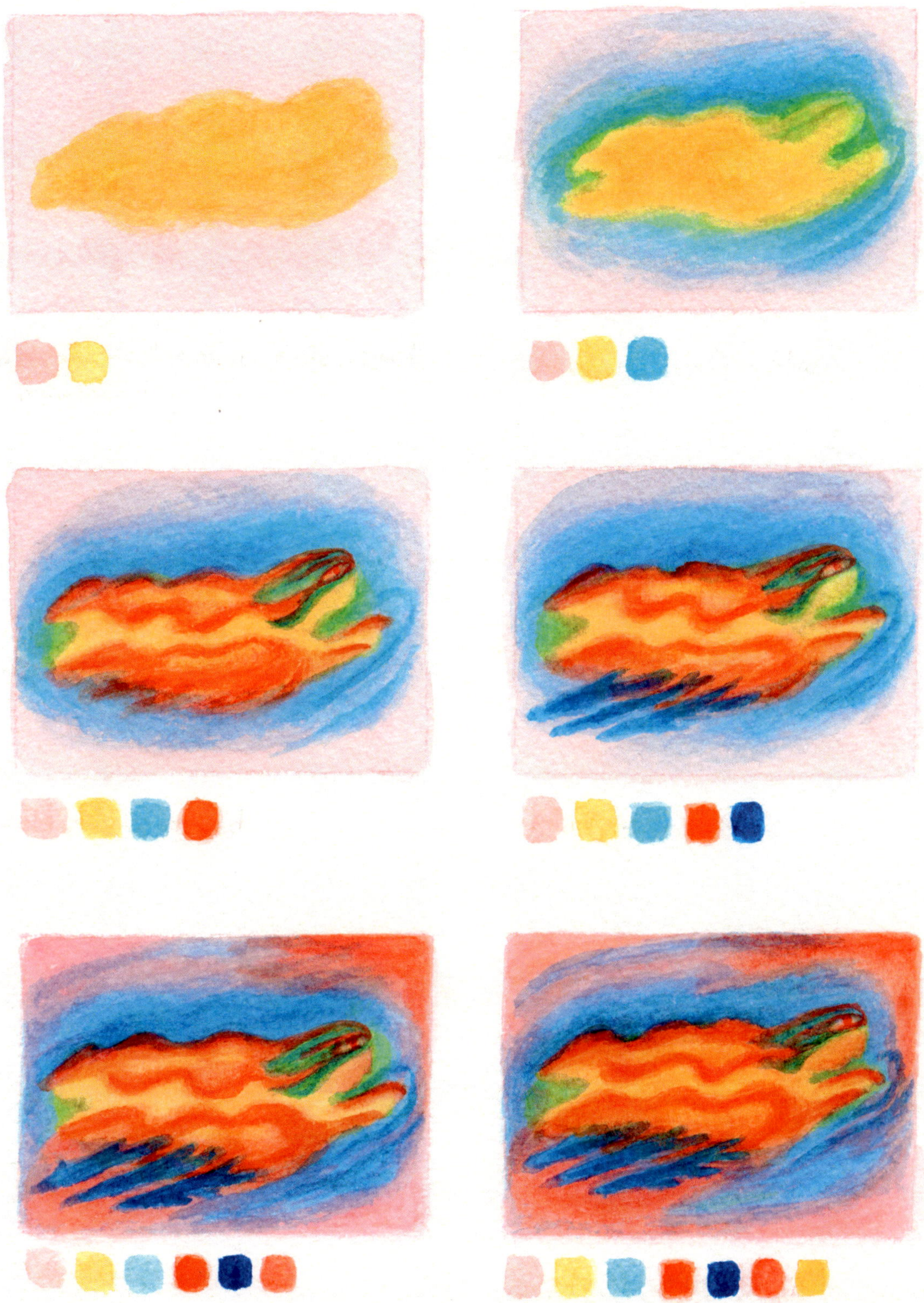

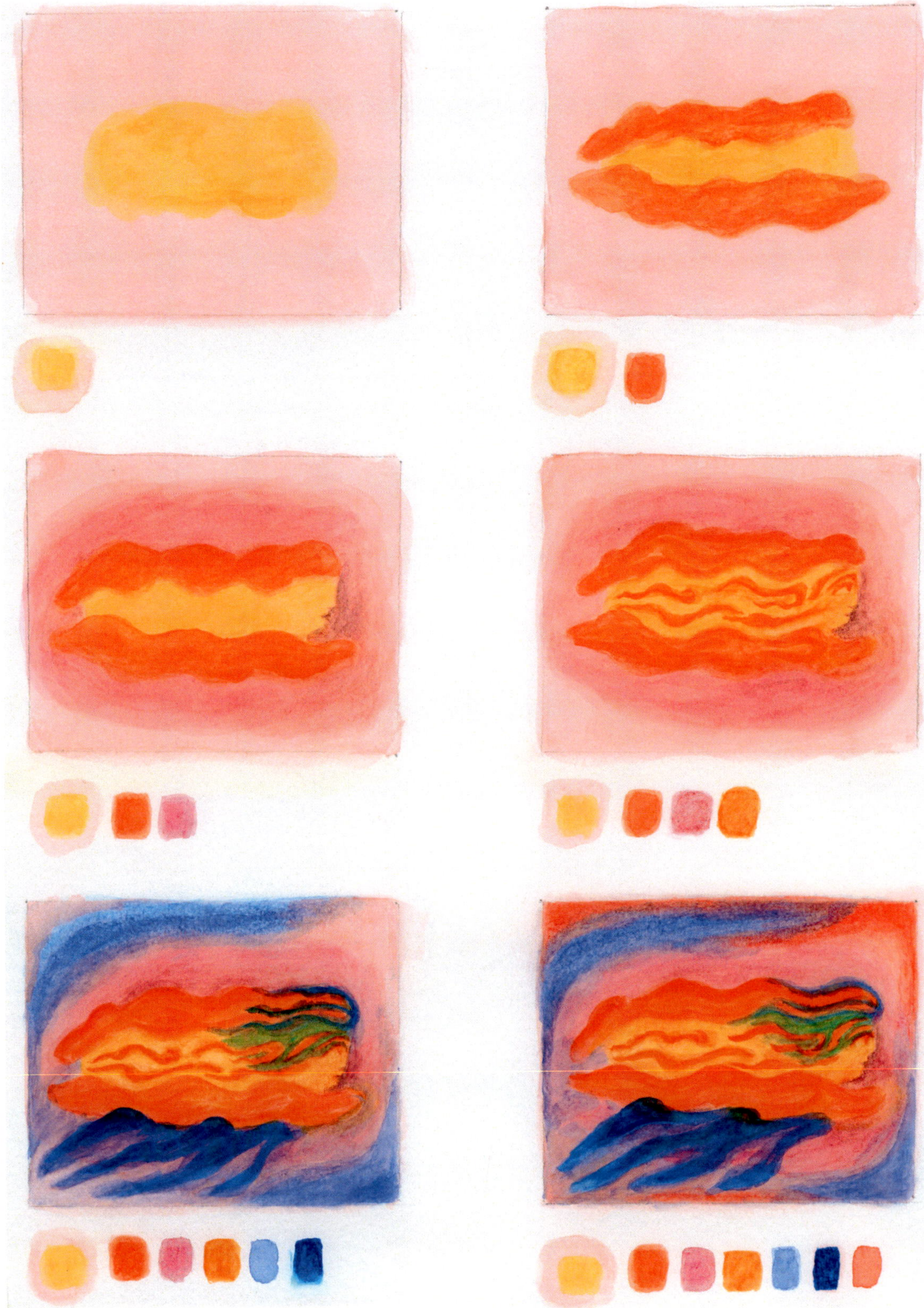

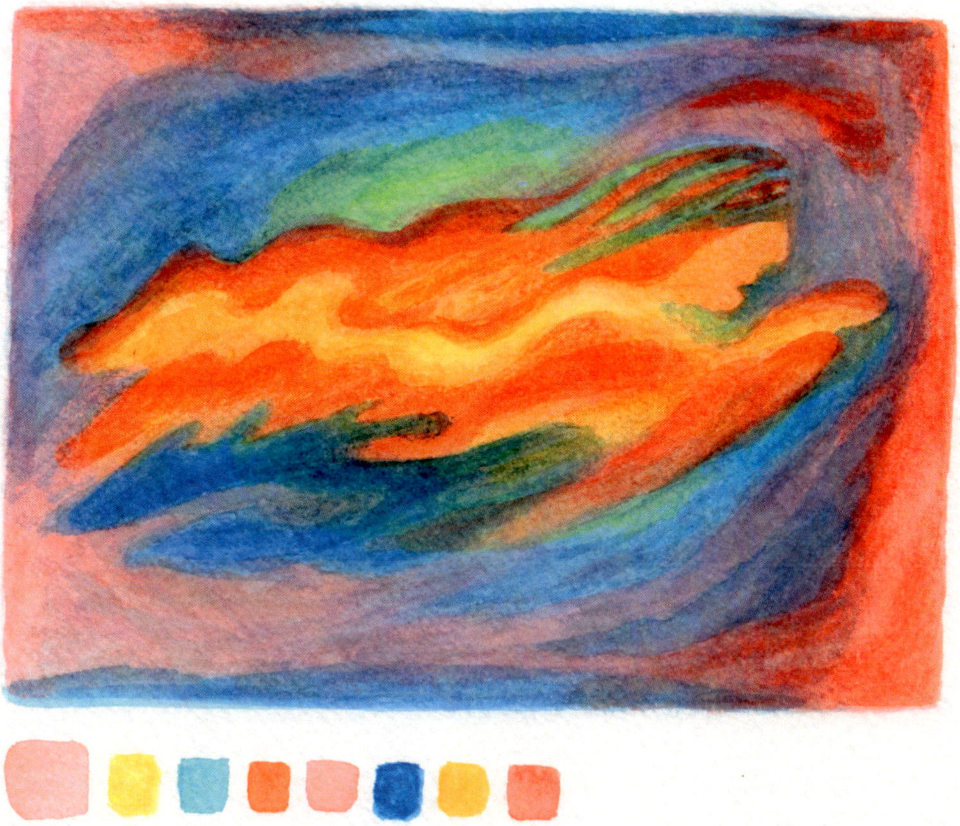

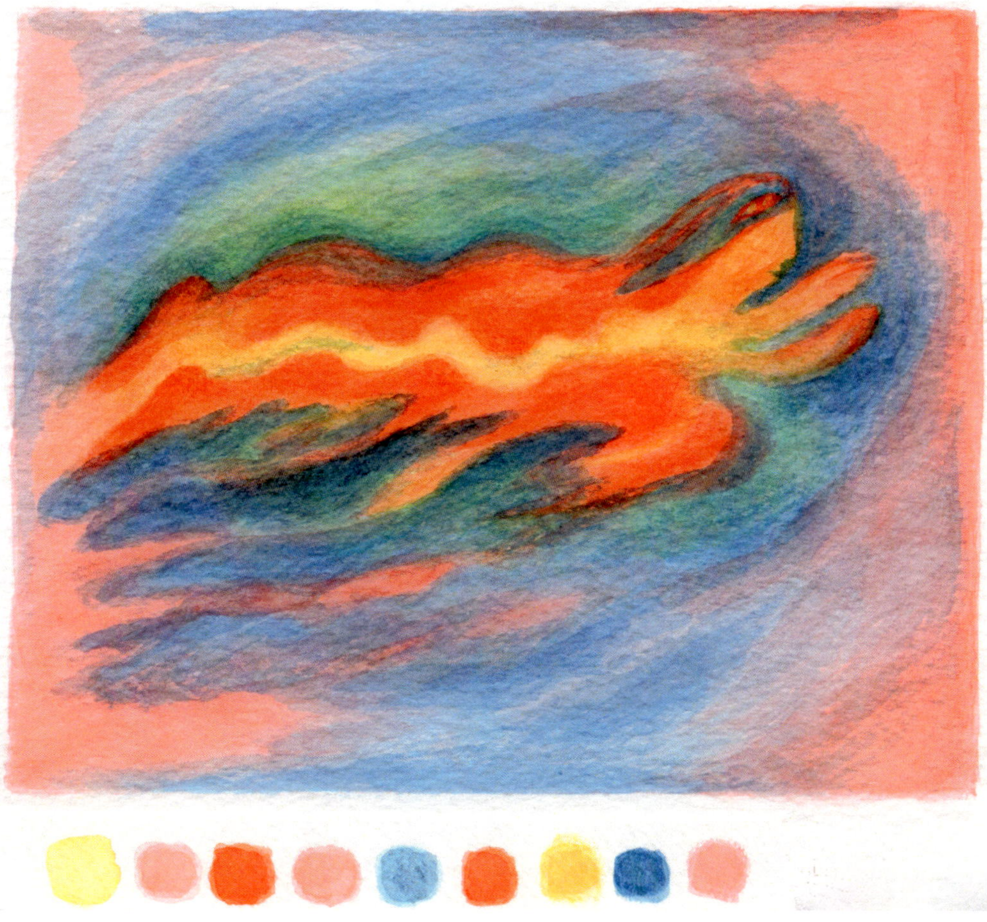

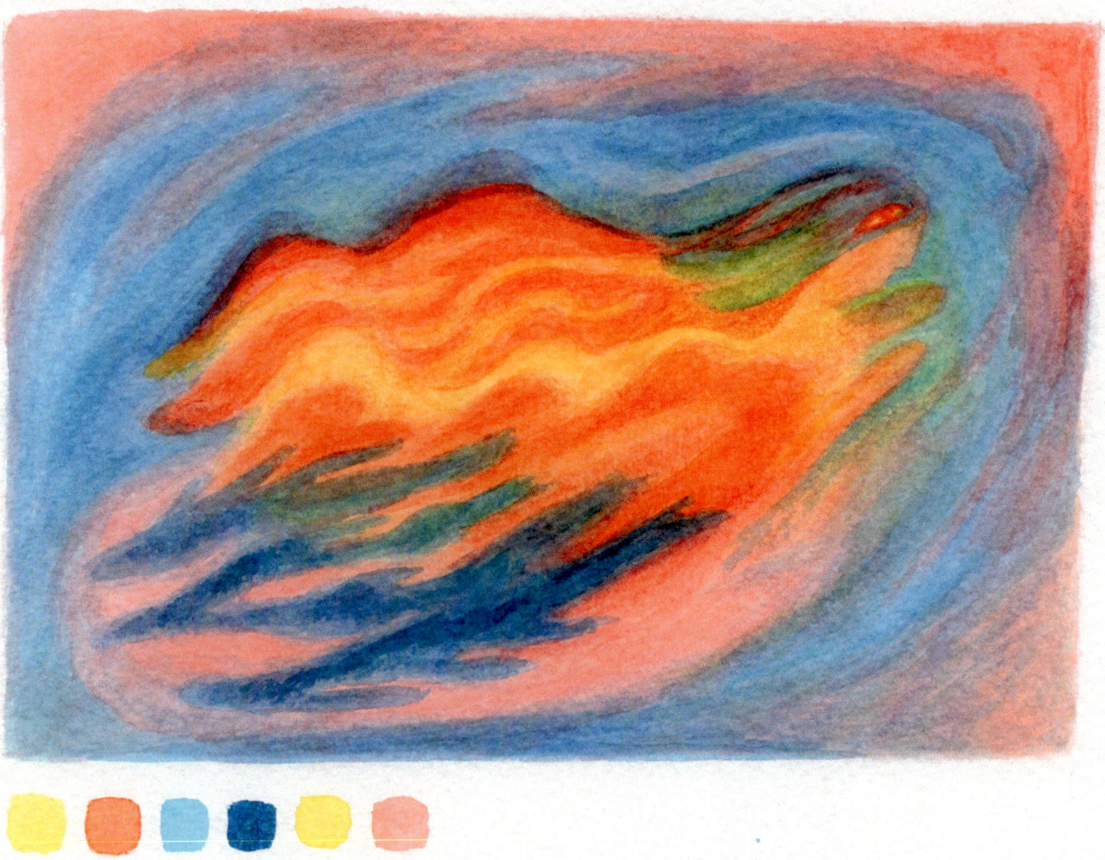

Chapter Two
An Approach to the Language of Colour

In the Archetypal Human-Animal motif we can see that the colours create dynamic polarities, which can be translated into a language of colour. Such a language consists of contrasting opposites, which in turn relate to the characteristics of the colours. For example, the darker mixed colours in the painting have the following characteristics:

dark
dense
mixed
heavy
substantial
opaque

These can be contrasted with the brighter, pure colours which have the following characteristics

bright/radiant
fine
pure
light
insubstantial
transparent

Such contrasting opposites are the 'building blocks', or fundamental principles, of our existence. The lists can be developed to cover a wide field:

hot – cold	above – below
warm – cool	centre – periphery
wet – dry	loud – soft
opening – closing	sweet – sour
expanding – contracting	harmonious – inharmonious
loosening – binding	long – short
active – passive	soft – hard

Considering colours in this way provides a balancing process through which a composition can be built up. If a painting becomes too one-sided, then an opposite polarity can balance it out.

The colours begin to 'speak' to us on another level, thus creating a rich colour-language that supports our colour-decisions. This colour-language enables us to enter more deeply into the colour-world, and to perceive the formative forces within the colours themselves.

Colour comes to life in a new way, enabling a whole new approach to aesthetics to be developed – aesthetics which are based upon an enlivened and an enlivening colour-process. Image, or motif, and colour are creatively united, and our paintings begin to resound to the sensitive onlooker.

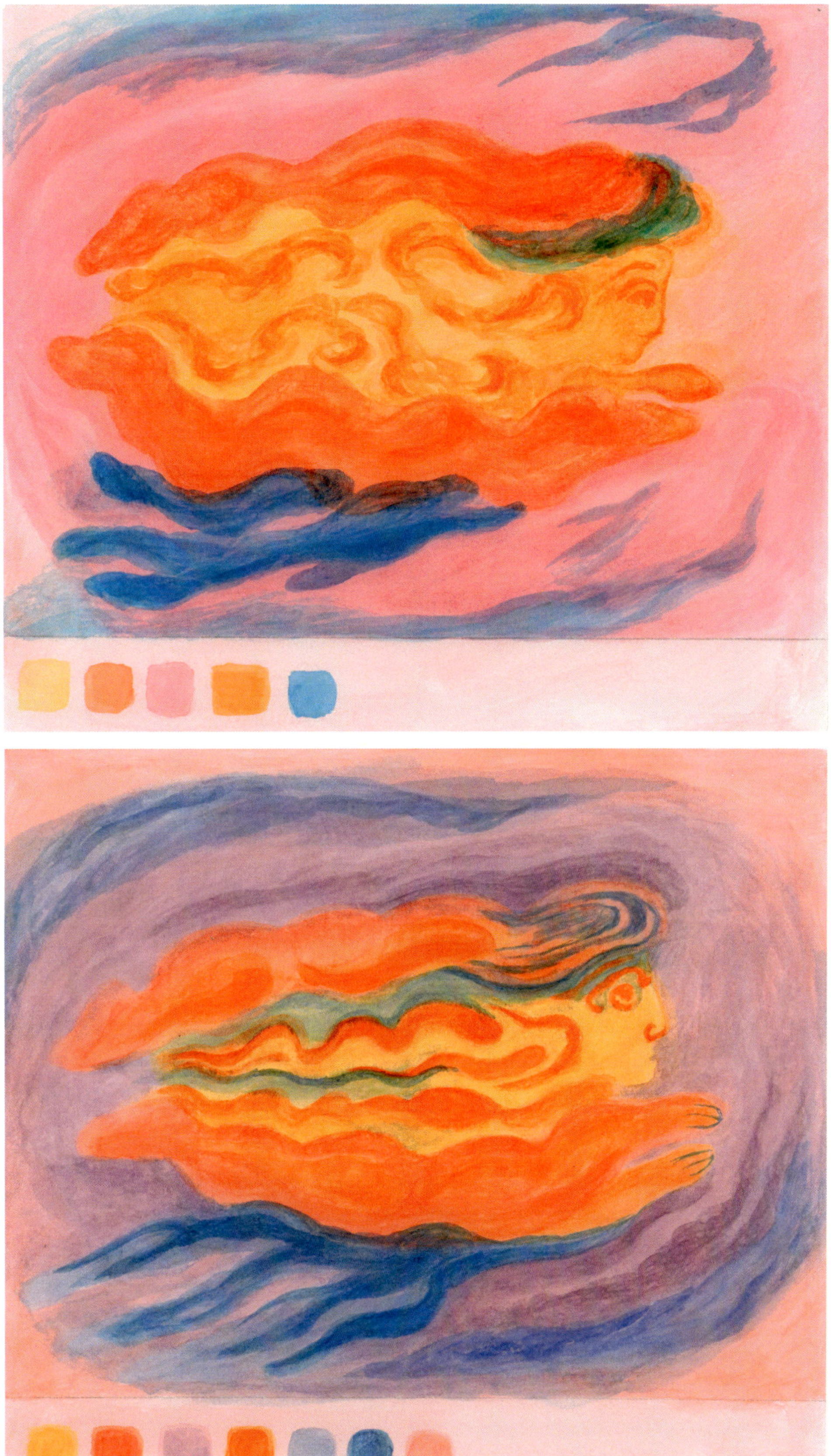

31.

APPENDICES

Appendix One
Summary of Evolutionary Phases

1. Ancient Saturn
A cosmic 'body' of spiritual warmth and formations of warmth. The gods, or higher spiritual beings, give of their own substance so that something akin to warmth arises within a space in the solar system, which will create a home for their development of humanity – their offspring. Only the Hierarchies exist, and the human being exists as a thought of these gods.*

> *Human Beings*: Were created as bodies of spiritual warmth within the divinity of the godhead. The archetypal foundations of the human body, in particular the human head formation, exist as flowing, weaving, surging warmth within the activity of the exalted spiritual beings. This fashioning of the prototype of a physical body was the first step of creation.
>
> *Animals*: An archetype of the future butterflies also enters into cosmic existence within the warmth activity.†
>
> *Minerals*: some of the substance of the Saturn condition, which was not irradiated, created the first spiritual beginnings of what would become the minerals.
>
> *Pralaya* – A state of dissolution and rest; a sleep of worlds.

2. Ancient Sun
A vast spiritual-etheric body, at first recapitulating the ancient Saturn condition; then processes of contraction and densification as warmth becomes radiant spiritual air. The entire sun-globe consists of shining luminous etheric warmth-forms. Higher spiritual beings endow these radiant human-warmth bodies with their etheric substance.

Spirits of Movement, Spirits of Form and Spirits of Personality work together with the Spirits of Love (the Seraphim).

> *Human beings*: A head and breathing organism composed only of what was of the nature of air, undulating and scintillating with light, created of warmth and delicate luminous etheric air substance.

---

* See Roy Wilkinson's helpful summary in: *Rudolf Steiner, An Introduction to his Spiritual World-View, Anthroposophy*: Chapter 4.

† See Rudolf Steiner's *Man as Symphony of the Creative Word*: Chapter V.

To the head formation was added the etheric archetype of the breathing and heart system, the rhythmic system, the beginnings of the nervous system and what would – aeons later – become the sense organs, were also given their etheric forms.

Animals: An archetype of the bird kingdom came into existence. Also the archetype of what would become the lion kingdom came into existence in relation to the human rhythmic system.*

Minerals: Substance resurrected from the Saturn-phase but not wholly transformed became the foundation substance of the future mineral kingdom.

Pralaya – A state of dissolution and rest; a sleep of worlds.

3. Ancient Moon

A recapitulation of the ancient Saturn and sun phases at a higher level. At first sun, moon and earth were united; then for a time the ancient sun separated to continue its own further evolution. Towards the final phase of ancient moon phase it reunited once more with the moon-earth, forming a single cosmic entity.

During the separation, a movement of the moon about the sun was induced so that alternating relations occurred. Human beings could experience the sublime and cosmic greatness of the sun-life, experiencing spiritual harmonies of truly divine music – universal harmonies which coursed through and gave shape to their astral bodies. When moon influences were stronger, human beings sensed the working of Angel beings, who were forming etheric groups of humans, thereby feeling their own sense of ego-hood reflected in the etheric nerves and senses of their human groups.

A delicate fluid watery element arose in which three differing kingdoms of human-animal, animal-vegetable and vegetable-soft mineral could develop in the vaporous atmosphere. All were worked upon by Spirits of Wisdom, the Kyriotetes.†

Human beings were created of soft, flowing sap-like fluid substances, with currents of air flowing through them. They had in their nature both plant and animal constituents. From the head projected etheric and astral bodies. They could inhale sublime cosmic substance from the majesty of the universe, and obtained a certain perfection of form. They were now entirely ethereal. Spiritual beings from both the sun and moon, worked upon them, which brought about alternating states of consciousness.‡

Gaseous substances had been condensed to watery ones so that, in addition to the head and breathing organism, now was added a rudimentary digestive

---

* Ibid.

† Rudolf Steiner, *An Outline of Esoteric Science*: Chapter Four.

‡ Ibid.

system. Humans now existed of a fluid head, rhythmic system and abdomen. Because ancient moon consisted of a water substance, the ethereal human beings had outgrowths which buoyed them up as they swam through the airy vaporous water.* They experienced the nearness of the spiritual beings who were sustaining them, feeling: 'this, my environment upholds me in existence'.†

Animals: In relation to the human abdominal digestive system, the archetype of the kingdom that was represented later by the cow came into being – that is, the animals predominantly adapted to digestion.‡

In the last phase of the ancient moon period, the archetypes of reptiles and amphibians came into being in very simple primal forms in connection with the human intestinal digestive system. This was followed by the fishes, also in delicate primordial forms, in relation to the nascent development of the human reproductive organs.§ It must be remembered that all creatures, including the human being, existed in an ephemeral non-solid condition.

Plants: Part of the Saturn substance affected by the etheric of the sun-phase would become the future plant-world.¶

Minerals: Part of the Saturn substance not vitalised would become the future mineral world.**

Pralaya – A state of dissolution and rest; a sleep of worlds.

4. Earth

The ancient earth was comprised of sun, moon and earth as etheric and astral substances. The first three phases were recapitulations of the Saturn, sun and moon phases, each at a higher level. All is soul and spirit, radiating soul-light (not even physical light, as we know it). In this world-entity is contained all that is potentially able to be metamorphosed into the many creatures of the future physical earth.††

The earth phase initially has a fiery nature, and includes the great beings of the sun within it. This is followed by an air-phase during which spiritual tones – cosmic harmonies – ring out. A third phase brings a watery substance and the subsequent separation

* Rudolf Steiner, *Man as Symphony of the Creative Word*, Lecture VI.

† Rudolf Steiner, *An Outline of Esoteric Science*: Chapter Four.

‡ Ibid.

§ Ibid.

¶ Roy Wilkinson, *Rudolf Steiner, An Introduction to his Spiritual World-View, Anthroposophy*: Chapter 4.

** Ibid.

†† Rudolf Steiner, *An Outline of Esoteric Science*, Chapter Four.

of the higher hierarchies. They later create the formation of the sun from where they can work, bringing about alternating times upon the earth.

Due to strong influences from the moon, which hardened processes on earth too rapidly, mighty spirits brought about the moon's separation from the earth. Then earth continues its evolutionary phases of Polaris, Hyperborea, Lemuria, Atlantis, and the Post-Atlantean epochs.

> *Human Beings*: During the first earth phase, human beings were still in astral form, as self-forms of large egg-like shapes, feeling warmth rising upwards into them from below, and etheric-air substance streaming around them.* After the sun's separation, they felt surging waves of sound helping them to shape and form themselves into delicate, plant and flower forms, which give the appearance of waving, fluttering flowers. Human beings lived within a blissful feeling of being shaped into such forms as these. They were fine and fragile, created of astral substance, like light-filled wraiths, diverse in form in different parts of the etherial earth-substance.†
>
> Gradually, the etheric body condensed to become a light-fire body, into which sun beings could breathe rarefied air. The streams of warmth would later become the blood circulation; the air became the foundation of breathing and also the basis of the nervous system.‡ Watery substances were added.
>
> Human beings began to diversify. A reflection of the inner soul-condition could be seen in the external bodily form. Some developed clearer head forms, others developed appendages. Due to the hardening processes taking place through the moon's influence, some human souls were brought to a different kind of life history and dwelt with high spiritual beings upon the various planetary bodies, which suited their further evolution.§
>
> Only the most mature, the strongest human souls, felt themselves equal to the task of transforming the earthly bodily form into the true human form, which was possible with the working of the Spirits of Form, and only after the separation of the moon. The 'I' flowed down through the generations, like a common consciousness.
>
> When human spiritual souls were sufficiently developed to be able to build themselves suitable bodies, the Spirits of Form, the Exusiai, endowed them with a spark of their own fire. The human 'I', the ego, was kindled.

* Ibid.

† Ibid.

‡ Ibid.

§ Ibid.

With the gradual descent, which is termed the Fall from Paradise, earthly life began.

Animals: Some of the living-feeling entities were not mature enough to receive an Ego. This gave rise to the animal kingdom, which consisted of physical, etheric and astral bodies only. They had souls which could not dwell in a single creature, but each group of a particular species shared one soul together, a group-soul.*

Plants: With the working together of the astral from the sun and the etheric of the earth, physical forms arose out of the watery element. These became the plant kingdom, which grew eventually into recognisable forms, gigantic in size, covering the surface of the earth.†

Minerals: As with the animals and the plants, the mineral kingdom also arose by being thrust out from the evolution of humanity. Its structures represent what was still left in a hardened condition when the moon separated from the earth. As earth continued to harden and condense, so also did the many metals and the many types of minerals.

* Ibid.

† Ibid.

Appendix Two

TIME CHART		EPOCHS OF EVOLUTION
	Purely spiritual existence	
Condensation as far as warmth-filled air.		Polarian
Condensation as far as air and warmth (gas)		Hyperborean
Separation of the earth-moon and the sun		
	Geology begins	
Pre-Cambrian	Thin liquid imbued with air and warmth. Gradual condensation of metals into liquids. Human being invisible; cloud-like.	Archaeon Early Lemurian (No fossil remains)
Cambrian	Foamy, jelly-like condition of the earth. Soft, malleable human beings.	
Ordovician	Paleozoic	
Silurian	(Paleolithic)	Primary Middle Lemurian (fishes)
Devonian		
Carboniferous	30,000 B.C.	
Permian	Gradual solidification of the earth	

Differentiation and separation of the moon from the earth.

Triassíc Jurassic Cretaceous	Mesozoic (Mesolithic) Swampy, fiery, wild, volcanic conditions. 10,000–8,000 BC	Secondary Later Lemurian (reptiles)
Eocene Oligocen Miocene Pliocene	Cainozoic (Cenozoic) 8,000–5,000 BC	Tertiary Atlantean Epoch (mammals)
Ice Ages Neolithic 5,000–4,000 BC Chalcolithic 4,000–3150 BC		Quaternary Post-Atlantean Epochs

Reference: 'Epochs of Evolution' by John Waterman, publ. in *The Golden Blade* 1957

TIME CHART — EPOCHS OF EVOLUTION

Eras	Periods or Systems			Principal Physical and Biological Features	
CENOZOIC	Quaternary	Recent	Mineralisation of earth	Glaciers retreat. Extinction of giant mammals. Atlantean races develop.	ATLANTEAN AGE
		Pleistocene		Glaciation. Giant mammals. First modern hominids in late Pleistocene.	
	Tertiary	Pliocene		Mammals specialise further. First ape-like hominids in Africa.	
		Miocene		Mammals acquire modern characters. Higher apes.	
		Oligocene		Many earlier mammalian forms become extinct. First apes and monkeys.	
		Eocene		Last great mountain uplift. Expansion of early mammals. Primitive horse.	
		Palaeocene		Great development of primitive mammals.	
MESOZOIC	Cretaceous			Saurians reach peak then become extinct. Early mammals still small and primitive.	LATE LEMURIAN
	Jurassic			Conifers and cycads dominant. Primitive birds. First mammals appear.	
	Triassic			Ferns and cycads dominant. Great expansion of reptiles, including early dinosaurs.	MIDDLE LEMURIAN AGE
PALEOZOIC	Permian			Ferns abundant; cycads and ammonites appear. Coral forests decline. Trilobite extinction. Reptiles surpass amphibians.	
	Carboniferous			Land plants diversify. Crinoids reach their peak. Amphibians abundant. Reptiles appear. Modern sharks develop. Few land animals.	
	Devonian		Mountain-building processes	Land plants evolving; large trees appear. Brachiopods reach their peak. Amphibians appear, also first sharks and insects. Primitive fish diversify.	EARLY LEMURIAN AGE
	Silurian			First small land plants. Corals and shelled cephalopods abundant. Primitive jawed fish appear. Trilobites decline.	
	Ordovician			Limestone deposited in shallow seas. Great expansion of marine invertebrates. Primeval jawless fish.	
	Cambrian			Shallow seas cover parts of continents. Trilobites and brachiopods abundant.	
PRE-CAMBRIAN	Upper Pre-Cambrian		Earth's crust soft	Metamorphic sedimentary rocks, lava flows and granitic rocks. Calcareous algae and invertebrates predominate.	
	Archaean			Gradually solidifying crust forms over fluid earth. Vitalised atmosphere. Primeval (etheric) plant and animal forms.	

Adapted from Webster's New World Dictionary, 1982
Time Chart
Source: "The Animals and their Destiny." Karl Konig

List of Illustrations

In colour:

Black and White Drawings:

H and I	Stone carvings of human	*After the Ice. A Global History* Human/ fish figures c. 6400 BC *20,000 BC–5000 BC* by Steven Mithen, University of Reading. Weidenfeld-Nicholson, London
J	Native drawing of a sea spirit. The Solomon Islands	*Mythology of all Races* Vol. 9
K	A composite creature	Stone carving. Ref: *God's Beasts*
L	Alchemical illustration.	*A Divine Magic* by Andre and Lynette Singer. Box Tree
M	The Anchor Cross with Fishes	*Christian Symbols, Ancient and Modern* by H. Child and D. Colles. Bell and Hyman. London
N	Fish with PX Monogram	As above

All drawings are by the author.

References and Suggested Reading

Rudolf Steiner:

The Apocalypse of St John, Anthroposophic Press, 2004

Atlantis. Texts compiled with introduction and commentary by Andrew Welburn. Sophia Books, 2007

Genesis, Biblical Secrets of Creation, Rudolf Steiner Press, 2002

Calendar of the Soul, Anthroposophic Press, 2007

Cosmic Memory, Atlantis and Lemuria, SteinerBooks, 2006

From Crystals to Crocodiles, Answers to Questions, Rudolf Steiner Press 2002

Goethe's World View, Mercury Press, 1985

The Influence of Spiritual Beings upon Man, Anthroposophic Press, 1982

The Michael Mystery, Anthroposophical Publishing Company, 1956

Mystery Knowledge and Mystery Centres, Rudolf Steiner Press, 1997

Nature's Open Secret, Anthroposophic Press, 2000

Occult Science, Rudolf Steiner Press, 2013

Supersensible Influences in the History of Mankind, Rudolf Steiner Press, 1956

Theosophy of the Rosicrucian, Rudolf Steiner Press, 1981

Universe, Earth and Man, Rudolf Steiner Press, 1987

Bibliography

Rudolf Steiner:

Blackboard Drawings 1919–1924. Edited by Walter Kugler. Rudolf Steiner Press, 2003

The Training Path for Painters, Rudolf Steiner Verlag, Dornach, Switzerland, 1986. (German title: *Ein malerischer Schulungsweg.*) A portfolio of coloured reproductions of Rudolf Steiner's paintings and pastel drawings

Other Authors:

Celtic Myths and Legends by Charles Squire, Lomond Books, 2000

Creation and Evolution by Paul Carline, *New View Magazine*, issue 42, Winter 2006/7

Dictionary of English Folklore by J. Simpson and S. Roud, Oxford University Press, 2000

Dictionary of World Folklore by Alison Jones, 1995

The Golden Bough, A Study of Magic and Religion by James Frazer, Penguin Books, 1996

The Language of Colour in the First Goethearnum, by Hilde Raske, Verlag Freies Geistesleben, 1983

The Little Mermaid by Hans Christian Andersen

Man and Animal, Their Essential Difference by Herman Poppelbaum, Anthroposophical Publishing Company, 1960

Man and Mammals: Towards a biology of Form by Wolfgang Schad, Waldorf Press, 1977

The Masks of God: Primitive Mythology by Joseph Campbell, Penguin Group, 1976

Mythology of the Babylonian People by Donald A. Mackenzie, Bracken Books, 1996

New Larousse Encyclopaedia of Mythology, Paul Hamlyn, 1968

Reincarnation and Other Essays by Dr Eugen Kolisko, Kolisko Archive, 1978

The World Guide to Gnomes, Fairies, Elves, and other Little People, Compendium of International Fairy Folklore by Thomas Keightly, Grameroy Books, 1978

The Animals and Their Destiny, A New View of Evolution. 12 lectures given by Karl König, Camphill Books, 1963